Another Day in Nazareth

ANOTHER DAY IN NAZARETH

BARRY BLACKSTONE

RESOURCE *Publications* • Eugene, Oregon

ANOTHER DAY IN NAZARETH

Copyright © 2018 Barry Blackstone. All rights reserved. Except for brief quotations in critical publications or reviews, no part of this book may be reproduced in any manner without prior written permission from the publisher. Write: Permissions, Wipf and Stock Publishers, 199 W. 8th Ave., Suite 3, Eugene, OR 97401.

Resource Publications
An Imprint of Wipf and Stock Publishers
199 W. 8th Ave., Suite 3
Eugene, OR 97401

www.wipfandstock.com

PAPERBACK ISBN: 978-1-5326-6495-3
HARDCOVER ISBN: 978-1-5326-6496-0
EBOOK ISBN: 978-1-5326-6497-7

Manufactured in the U.S.A.   11/15/18

I DEDICATE THIS JOURNAL OF JESUS TO A MAN IN MY NAZARETH THAT HELPED ME SEE THE VALUE OF LIVING IN A SMALL TOWN!
MAX HOLTS OWNED THE LOCAL STORE AND ATTENDED MY HOME CHURCH. MAX GAVE HIS LIFE TO SERVING THE PEOPLE OF PERHAM AND WAS A FINE EXAMPLE OF WHAT IT TAKES TO LIVE "ANOTHER DAY IN NAZARETH."

CONTENTS

Other Books of Barry Blackstone | ix
Acknowledgement | xi

Prelude: Another Day in Nazareth | 1
A Morning in Nazareth | 4
The Hills of Nazareth | 6
The Flowers of Nazareth | 8
The Terrain of Nazareth | 10
A Mountainside in Nazareth | 12
A Homecoming at Nazareth | 14
A Father in Nazareth | 16
A Peace Over Nazareth | 18
A Hope in Nazareth | 20
The Sky Over Nazareth | 22
Solitude From Nazareth | 24
A Craftsman in Nazareth | 26
Dew on Nazareth | 28
The Moon Over Nazareth | 30
A Moonset Over Nazareth | 32
A Concert Near Nazareth | 34
A Rain in Nazareth | 36
A Reflection About Nazareth | 38
A Storm Over Nazareth | 40
A Succourer in Nazareth | 42
The Creed of Nazareth | 44
The Community of Nazareth | 46

Sleeping in Nazareth | 48
Downtown in Nazareth | 50
A Simplicity to Nazareth | 52
A Rainbow Over Nazareth | 54
Sisters in Nazareth | 56
A Bark in Nazareth | 58
An Oak in Nazareth | 60
A Harvest Nazareth | 62
A Cedar in Nazareth | 64
A Seed in Nazareth | 66
The Steadfastness of Nazareth | 68
The Spring of Nazareth | 70
The Ridge of Nazareth | 72
A Rooster in Nazareth | 74
A Wind in Nazareth | 76
The Crickets of Nazareth | 78
The Ants of Nazareth | 80
A Ploughing in Nazareth | 82
A Shower in Nazareth | 84
Clouds Over Nazareth | 86
Laughing in Nazareth | 88
An Autumn in Nazareth | 90
A Hen in Nazareth | 92
Waiting in Nazareth | 94
Alone in Nazareth | 96
A Swallow in Nazareth | 98
The Granite of Nazareth | 100
Hummingbirds Over Nazareth | 102
Fruitless in Nazareth | 104
An Escape From Nazareth | 106
Patience in Nazareth | 108
Night in Nazareth | 110
Content in Nazareth | 112
The Philosophy of Nazareth | 114
Thorns in Nazareth | 116
The Wildflowers of Nazareth | 118
The Country of Nazareth | 120
A Jaunt Through Nazareth | 122

A Remembrance of Nazareth | 124
The Crossroad of Nazareth | 126
A Path in Nazareth | 128
A Dawn in Nazareth | 130
Boyhood in Nazareth | 132
Barefoot in Nazareth | 134
Daybreak in Nazareth | 136
The Pageantry of Nazareth | 138
The Landscape of Nazareth | 140
The Bible of Nazareth | 142
An Illustration From Nazareth | 144
Wings Over Nazareth | 146
Caring in Nazareth | 148
Cheerfulness in Nazareth | 150
An Example of Nazareth | 152
Workmanship in Nazareth | 154
The Salt of Nazareth | 156
The World of Nazareth | 158
The Code of Nazareth | 160
A Sabbath in Nazareth | 162
The Butter of Nazareth | 164
Home-Life in Nazareth | 166
A Nazarene in Nazareth | 168
The Nazarenes of Nazareth | 170
The Honey of Nazareth | 172
Workshop in Nazareth | 174
Counselor of Nazareth | 176
A Sowing Sermon From Nazareth | 178
Twilight in Nazareth | 180
Scraping in Nazareth | 182
A Tourist in Nazareth | 184
A Prayer From Nazareth | 186
A Petition from Nazareth | 188
Respect From Nazareth | 190
The Kingdom Started in Nazareth | 192
The Will of Nazareth | 194
Daily Bread in Nazareth | 196
Forgiveness in Nazareth | 198

Temptation in Nazareth | 200
Deliverance From Nazareth | 202
Postlude: Jesus of Nazareth | 204

OTHER BOOKS OF BARRY BLACKSTONE

Though None Go With Me
Rendezvous in Paris
Though One Go With Me
Scotland Journey
The Region Beyond
Enlarge My Coast
From Dan to Beersheba and Beyond
The Uttermost Part
Homestead Homilies
Rover: A Boy's Best Friend
North to Alaska and Back

ACKNOWLEDGEMENT

I WOULD NOT HAVE gotten this book project finished if not for the editing, typing, and compiling of and by my dear friend Rosemary Campbell, our church's pianist. I would like to thank her for the hours and days she spent reading and correcting the errors in the original manuscript.

Prelude

ANOTHER DAY IN NAZARETH

MATTHEW 2:23—AND HE CAME and dwelt in a city call Nazareth: that it might be fulfilled which was spoken by the prophets, He shall be called a Nazarene.

I once dreamed of pastoring a big church in a big place and making a big difference. As I near my 60th spiritual birthday (June 4, 2018), my dreams and desires have changed.

I haven't and will never pastor a big church. I haven't and will not live in a big place. And as for making a big difference, the verdict is still out. What has made this dramatic change in my basic philosophy? It all happened quite suddenly when I came to the realization that my dear Lord and Saviour Jesus Christ had lived nearly ninety percent of His life on earth in Nazareth!

Remember what Nathanael said to Philip when hearing Philip's testimony about finding the Messiah: *"Can there any good thing come out of Nazareth?"* (John 1:46) How often have we thought that greatness is geographical? Because a man is born in a big place where he finds great opportunities for advancement that is the reason he becomes important. Greatness however does not depend on location, or largeness. When Alexander marched out of the insignificant Greek province of Macedonia there were those who probably said, "Can any one great come out of Macedonia?" And yet before he was done, he would be known as Alexander the

ANOTHER DAY IN NAZARETH

Great of Macedonia. Most would have thought he should have come from Athens or Sparta, but greatness is not geographical!

Greatness also doesn't take into consideration how long one stays in Nazareth. I see now that I have spent most of my nearly seventy years in Nazareth or places like Nazareth. I was born in a small farming community in northern Maine. In the first century in Galilee Nazareth was a typical farming village where agriculture determined nearly every aspect of daily life—just like in Perham, Maine. Jesus' boyhood home was located in a sheltered basin nearly 1300 feet above sea level. Perham is also located in hill country just above the Aroostook River Valley. My four pastorates have taken me to rural hamlets in southern New Hampshire, back to northern Maine, to a small island off the down east coast of Maine, and now to the riverside (Union River) and seaside (Gulf of Maine) town of Ellsworth. Even in His hometown Jesus was trying to demonstrate to the world that God looks at people, not places! I like this from an unknown poet:

"Father, where shall I work today, and my love flow warm and free? He pointed out a tiny spot and said, tend that place for me. I answered him quickly, Oh, no! Not that! Why no would ever see, no matter how well my work was done; not that little place for me! The word he spoke then wasn't stern; he answered me tenderly: Nazareth was a little place, and so was Galilee."

Nazareth was the extent of Jesus' life for the bulk of His life. Just three short years were given to ministries among the "multitudes," and thirty years were given to the "few." I too have spent my life among individuals, small groups, and tiny congregations. For years I thought I was somehow losing out, wasting my time, accomplishing little. Then it came to me like a revelation—what of Jesus' time in Nazareth? It was then I began to ponder just how blessed a life I have had, a life much like Jesus' life. Who better to know what "another day in Nazareth" is like then one who has spent most of his days in small country towns. I have often speculated what the "silent" years in Nazareth were like for Jesus. Then it came to me—much like my days.

Dr. J. H. Jowett writes: "Our Lord Jesus lived for thirty years amid the happenings of the little town of Nazareth. Little villages spell out their stories in small events. And He, the young Prince of Glory, was in the carpenter's shop. He moved amid humdrum tasks, petty cares, village gossip, trifling trade, and He was faithful in that which was least. If these smaller things in life afford such riches of opportunity for the finest loyalty, all of our lives are wonderfully wealthy in possibility and promise. Even though our house is furnished with commonplace, it can be the house of the Lord all the days of our lives." Once I realized that my Lord had called me to "His lifestyle," I became more content, more confident, more thankful, and more determined to be found faithful in my Nazareth.

Nettie Rooker put it this way: "When I am tempted to repine that such a lowly lot is mine, there comes to a voice which saith 'Mine were the streets of Nazareth.' So mean, so common and confined, and He the monarch of mankind, yet patiently He traveleth those narrow streets of Nazareth. It may be I shall never rise to place of fame beneath the skies but walk in straitened ways till death narrow as the streets of Nazareth. But if through honor's arch I tread and there forget to bend my head, ah, let me hear the voice which saith 'Mine were the streets of Nazareth.'" It is with this message ringing in my ear and singing in my heart that I give you this series of thoughts on "Another Day in Nazareth." My goal is to share with you the experiences of my own life that I feel might have paralleled the life of Christ in Nazareth. I have determined to write each as a diary entry or a journal so that you my reader might use them to challenge yourself in your Nazareth days.

Most of us will never know the greatness of a great accomplishment, the creation of something totally new, or the success of changing the world like Christ did. But we all can experience "Another Day in Nazareth." Let us come to the conclusion that our best days will probably be our Nazareth days, and that there is service to be done; there is duty to be performed; and there are people to be helped even in Nazareth. "Can any good thing come out of 'Another Day in Nazareth?'" I will let you be the judge.

Barry Blackstone, February 7, 2018

A MORNING IN NAZARETH

Genesis 1:5 ... the morning ... the first day.

What was it like for the Creator to wake to his first morning in Nazareth? He who had created "morning," saw His creation through human eyes versus divine vision.

Luke tells us that Jesus grew at a normal rate (Luke 2:40,52) so He experienced many a morning as a child seeing and experiencing things for the first time—not as God but as boy; not as the Inventor, but as a spectator; not as Maker, but as man. "Morning had broken" and Jesus was off to explore His old world through His new human emotions of sight and sound and smell.

Eleanor Farjeon certainly did put it best when she wrote: "Morning has broken like the first morning; blackbird has spoken like the first bird. Praise for the singing! Praise for the morning! Praise for the springing fresh from the Word!" The God of the universe had been there on that first morning and now He was living it again through the senses of a child. Do you remember your first experiences when a morning brought high adventure and thrilling encounters? Jesus had left Heaven in the midst of a mid-summer's day's dream and had woken on earth to a bleak mid-winter's night's day. How long did it take Him to adjust to animals instead of angels, people instead of perfection, and time instead of eternity?

Jesus heard the birds He had created for the sky, the rooster He had created to signal the new day, and the other farm animals all lifting their voices to the rising sun. The air was warm and refreshing and the smell of wood smoke was in his room, and did he ask "Where am I?" "Sweet the rain's new fall sunlit from heaven, like the first dew fall on the first grass. Praise for the sweetness of the wet garden, sprung in completeness where His feet pass." Jesus had been to Nazareth before for He had created the limestone ridge that defines the southernmost border of lower Galilee. It seemed different viewing it from below rather than above. It carried with it a new sensation only known to One who knew He had been there before, but it felt so new. It was a new morning for the boy Jesus, and Nazareth was filled with paths that must be explored and examined.

As Jesus watched his first sunrise in Nazareth through human eyes, was he impressed with the strange tree line? (No "tree of life" along a flowing stream here.) Was he touched with the freshness of the landscape so foreign to what he was use to in a celestial meadow? Did he begin to sing "Mine is the sunlight! Mine is the morning, born of the one light Eden's saw play! Praise with elation, praise every morning, God's recreation of the new day!" What was in his heart and on His mind that first morning in Nazareth? Could it have been "This is the day I have made: I will rejoice and be glad in it?" (Psalms 118:24)

THE HILLS OF NAZARETH

PSALMS 121:1 I WILL lift up mine eyes unto the hills . . .

Of all the terrain variations on this planet, the Eternal Son chose to live the bulk of his life on earth in hill country. Have you ever pondered why?

From the summit of the village of Nazareth (the very "brow of the hill" from which the citizens of Nazareth would one day try to cast the Christ off-Luke 4:29), the boy Jesus could look west and see Mount Carmel on the Mediterranean coast where Elijah confronted the prophets of Baal (I Kings 18). When Jesus turned and took in the view to his east, he could see Mount Tabor where Barak's forces gathered to defeat the mighty Canaanite General Sisera (Judges 4). Looking northward, Jesus could see in the distance the snow-covered peak of Mount Hermon under whose shadow Joshua won a great battle during the conquest of Canaan (Joshua 11). Nazareth itself was founded in hill country so it was to this place the Christ settled after his Egyptian journey.

Only those born in hill country can understand the draw of home hills. Over the years I too have travelled in various directions from my home in Perham. One of my favorite trips was with my father-in-law, Stacy Meister, to fish the mighty Miramichi River in Canada. Each time we went we travelled back and forth across the hilly Renuos Highway. More often than not we would return with a cooler full of fish and many a fish story to tell. As we started our climb back over the hills of central New Brunswick, it was from a certain peak that we could see the hills of home, distant hazy hills, but our first glimpse of America after a few days in a foreign land. Despite the desire to stay, there is something about the sight of home, even if it is only a distant hill. Did Jesus find such strength in the hills surrounding his earthly home when he travelled away?

THE HILLS OF NAZARETH

I too come from the hills of northern Maine and though I live on the coast of Maine now, I still see the hills of home as a welcome sign. (It is sad, but there are many people that see God only as some distant, hazy "being" sitting on some throne in deep space.) The difference between the two is that I have climbed those hills and explored those valleys. I believe Jesus climbed and explored the hilltops as I did, and I found what he found. Hill country is a wonderful place to spend time with God and find Him to be personal, not distant. We know of the intimate relationship that Jesus had with his Father while on earth. That unique bond was established in Heaven and continued in Galilee. The Psalmist wrote it, but Jesus practiced it from the hills of Nazareth. When you know the Father as Jesus knew the Father, even a distant glimpse was like being by His side. Why did the Godhead pick the hill country of Nazareth for the Son to spend His childhood? They chose the high hills that we might learn "from whence cometh my help. My help cometh from the Lord . . . " (Psalms 121:1)

THE FLOWERS OF NAZARETH

Song of Solomon 2:12 The flowers appear on the earth . . .

When Jesus became the preacher of Galilee, he often used practical illustrations to highlight a point he was trying to get across. Sometimes he pointed to the flowers (Matthew 6:28, 29) He had created the flowers he saw in abundance on the slopes around Nazareth.

Every spring, after the grass turned green on the side hills surrounding the village of Nazareth, flowers began to blend their way into the pastures of Nazareth. Along the caravan route, Nazareth's gentle terrain and strategic location had made it a crossroad of trade and travel from earliest times, and around the fields of Nazareth grew such native wildflowers as tulips, hyacinths, irises, anemones, and narcissus, not to mention "the rose of Sharon" and "the lilies of the field." Jesus would also have seen the dandelion spreading its carpet of yellow. Now for those who think dandelions are only weeds, think again. They are God's spring flower. Be honest now, wasn't a bouquet of dandelions the first flowers you ever gave to your mother? Wasn't it a bunch of dandelions you first presented to that special girlfriend when you were young? It is sad to me that people spend so much time trying to kill spring's most beautiful flower. Did Jesus love dandelions?

In my mind's eye, I can see Jesus playing in the first heat of spring. The sky is a brilliant spring blue, and the white puffy clouds are as white as white can be. The wind is warm in his face as he flies across the green carpet in the back of his home. He stumbles and falls, and he looks up into the face of a dandelion. Remember, he is only five and the world of a five year old is huge. As he looks around, he notices this gigantic dandelion isn't alone. It seems there are hundreds of the sun-like plants surrounding him. They appear to be advancing, so he attacks. As quick as he can he begins to pick them, but soon his little hands are full, and he hasn't even dented their front line. With both hands overflowing, he begins to roll. Over and over he goes trying to stem their advancing tide. He stops and laughs and rolls some more until he lays exhausted on his back looking up into that endless blue sky. It is then he notices his hands are still full of flowers. His mind forms one word—MOTHER.

As quick as he can, he jumps to his feet. His focus is on the back door to the kitchen. By the time he reaches Mary's side, he presents to his boyhood queen two bouquets of dandelions. As if receiving the world's most expensive gift, Mary rewards Jesus with a kiss and a hug. That night as Jesus sits at the dining room table for supper; his eyes can't seem to stop looking at the pot of yellow flowers sitting in the middle of table.

THE TERRAIN OF NAZARETH

DEUTERONOMY 1: 7 TURN you, and take your journey, and go to the mount of the Amorites, and unto the places nigh thereunto, in the plain, in the hills, and in the vale . . .

Have you ever considered that when God told Jesus to leave Heaven that He was sending him to Nazareth? When the Eternal Spirit described the Promised Land to Moses recorded in the verse printed above, he was describing Nazareth. Besides the hills to the east, west, and north of Nazareth, south of Nazareth stretches the fertile Plain and Valley of Esdraelon (or the Plains of Jezreel) just ten miles southeast of Nazareth.

Jesus had come to the crossroads of history. This strategic location had been a battleground for most of the world's conquerors. The caravan route from Egypt, the road that no doubt Mary and Joseph had travelled when they brought the boy Jesus back to Nazareth (Matthew 2:22), crossed there. The caravan route from Damascus also crossed there. The caravan route from the King's Highway that ran the length of the Jordan River Valley had a northern east/west route that crossed there. Even in Jesus home town, he was being placed in the very place that the nations of the world crossed every day. "Another Day in Nazareth" was never just another day in Nazareth because of where Nazareth was located, the strategic crossroads of three continents.

"Going, but not knowing" is a terrible command to most. Few are the believers who will go without knowing where they are going, and yet that is exactly what God would have us do. But what I have learned about my God is that He will not send a country boy to a city, and He will not send a mountain man to a plain. It was not by chance or circumstance that Jesus was sent to Nazareth because even in the Old Testament the God of the Hebrews was known as a hill God. "And there came a man of God, and

THE TERRAIN OF NAZARETH

spake unto the king of Israel, and said, thus saith the Lord, because the Syrians have said, the Lord is God of the hills, but He is not God of the valleys, therefore will I deliver this entire great multitude into thine hand, and ye shall know that I am the Lord." (I Kings 20:28) The popular misconception of the Syrians is still alive and well being proclaimed by man to this day. Jesus came to the diverse terrain of Nazareth to prove that he was God over hills and mountains, vales and valleys, plains and pasture land.

Before I left for India in 2006, I asked my host, Shibu Simon, what was the terrain I would be heading into. It was in Edayappara, Kerala, where I learned the precept I have printed—"God will not send a country boy to the city, and God will not send a mountain man to a plain." When I left my home in Maine for India not really knowing where I was going, little did I know that I too was heading home? Can a man have two homes? Jesus did—Nazareth and Heaven.

A MOUNTAINSIDE IN NAZARETH

MATTHEW 21:11 ... THIS is Jesus the prophet of Nazareth ...

Nazareth's history goes back 2000 years before Jesus arrived. The first settlers were drawn by the sheltered mountainside that overlooked the lush Jezreel Valley. There was also found on that hillside a sweet spring (interestingly it is called Mary's Well today) of water. Thirty miles to the west was the Mediterranean Sea and fifteen miles to the east was the Sea of Galilee. Having been raised in the foothills of Aroostook County, Maine, I know of the lure of the other side of the hill. I have hiked along many a hilly trail, and the thrill is always around the next bend, around the next corner, around the next curve. Did Jesus love the thrill of seeing what was coming up the caravan road, just a stone's throw from downtown Nazareth?

Anticipation is the true spirit of the other side of the hill. What we know and have seen often becomes dull and drab. Our daily paths often lose their glamour and glitter as we repeat our walk. The other side of the hill with its uncertainty and unexpected sights draws us onward and upward as we search for that illusive change in life.

God has created our lives much like the hilly trails around Nazareth. How terrible would be our lives if it were just one long straight track. I remember in 1972 travelling on the straightest railroad track in the world—300 miles of straight rail without a dip or a diversion to the right or the left. I was travelling across the Gibson Desert in Western Australia. It was the most boring time of my ten week trip to Australia, and I had to retrace it on my way home. Boring! So is life without its curves and bends and corners. We might not be able to see down the road, but that is what makes life the adventure that it is. We never know what is coming up, but we can know the One that knows.

Vance Havner has written, "Indeed, that is what faith is: confidence in the other side of the hill. We know so little of life, of truth, of God and destiny. Business crashes, health fails, friends depart, cherished dreams collapse—yet somehow . . . most carry on. It is the other side of the hill that does it." Who of us hasn't thought to ourselves, "Well, next year be better? Will, tomorrow hold the answer? Will I feel okay next month?" All those questions are of the other side of the hill. So with our knapsack over our shoulder and our walking stick in our hand, we press on and push forward. Our goal? It's the other side of the hill. It may be a hill of pain, of loss, of disappointment, but we just know once we are over it, or around it, there lies on the other side of the hill a glorious meadow, a babbling brook, or a golden sunset.

For Christ of Nazareth, there remained the last hill. The world called it death, but Jesus revealed the resurrection and the life on the other side of the hill.

A HOMECOMING AT NAZARETH

MATTHEW 2:22, 23 . . . He turned aside into the parts of Galilee: and He came and dwelt in a city call Nazareth . . .

There is no indication that Jesus ever came to Nazareth until after spending the first few years of his life on the road. Following the death of King Herod, Joseph was told he could return to Israel in safety. After spending many years hiding out in a foreign land, it must have felt good for Mary and Joseph to come home (Luke 1:26), to rejoin family and friends, and to get back into the comfort of home. Having been in the pastorate for 45 years now, I know what it means to move. Night has come, and I am in my fourth church study in four and a half decades. It is quiet, and it is times like this I think of home. As Jesus settled into Nazareth, did he at times think of "home?"

As I type the word home into my personal computer, my mental computer begins to flash back to a HOME that has all but changed except in my memory. The word floats through my mind as a pleasant place where the crickets still chirp and the frogs still croak in the cool night air. The house on the Russell Place has still got an open porch under which I created my own little world. My trucks and tractors still farm that small field hid away behind Mother's flower bed. The garage is a wood shed again, and Rover can still be seen chasing cats in front of the old barn which burned many years ago, but in my mind's eye it still stands tall and strong in a stiff evening breeze. Sparrows and swallows by the hundreds still make their nests in that grand old barn, at least from where I am looking. And there is my beautiful sister Sylvia coming to get me. "Mum says it's too dark," she says. So we head into the house. It must be time for bed.

We live in an age where one's roots are said to be important yet many don't even know who their parents are. But I know of roots. I know what

A HOMECOMING AT NAZARETH

a home really is. I was raised on a homestead, a real homestead. My great-great-great grandfather Hartson Blackstone carved my home out of the virgin woods of Perham in 1861. My younger brother Jay was the sixth generation farmer to till that land. From father to son to father to son six times, imagine it if you can. Roots like that go deep, deep into your very soul. No force this side of heaven itself can root out that kind of home feeling. Surely, Jesus felt that way about heaven. As he settled into the routine that was Nazareth, did he start singing in his heart, "This world is not my home, I'm just passing through . . ."

Nazareth was Jesus' earthly home, but it never became his ultimate home. There must have been a homecoming when Joseph's family arrived from Egypt, but I can only imagine in the heart of their boy was the anticipation and expectation of the homecoming that would take place when the Son of God returned home to heaven!

A FATHER IN NAZARETH

LUKE 2:48 . . . BEHOLD; thy father and I sought thee sorrowing.

Few men have two fathers, but Jesus did. There was the heavenly Father and the Nazareth father. In my belief, I have come to the conclusion that the eternal Godhead picked carefully the man that would be in charge of the baby and eventually the boy Jesus. Joseph of Nazareth was chosen (Matthew 1:18–25) as Mary of Nazareth was chosen (Luke 1:26–38). Have you wondered about this Nazarene father?

Did Joseph instruct the boy Jesus in his boyhood by his example? Joseph was always there as Jesus grew from the baby of Bethlehem to the young man of Nazareth. Biblically, we can trace the life of Joseph from Jesus' conception (Matthew 1:20) to Jesus' twelfth year (Luke 2:41–52). After that Joseph is missing from the text. Most believe Joseph died before Jesus actually started his preaching and healing ministries. Throughout Jesus' boyhood Joseph was his father, but Jesus never forgot, "I must be about my Father's business" (Luke 2:49). Joseph was there for him.

I can see Joseph standing by that old carpenter's bench as Jesus returned from classes at the synagogue. I can hear Joseph singing the Psalms as he made a table for the neighbor while Jesus helped him. Can't you imagine Joseph sharing with Jesus the story of his birth and the arrival of the shepherds? I too have such an early father in Wendell E. Blackstone. It is wonderful to know that despite the changes in this world, there was still someone who for 93 years was (my earthly father passed into glory in 2017) a faithful steward of the homestead, a faithful husband to his wife, a faithful father to his five children, a faithful grandfather to his eight grandchildren, and a faithful deacon to his church.

I want; as I know Jesus did, to thank my father for what he did for me over the years and what he was to me over the years. I want to thank him

A FATHER IN NAZARETH

for showing me that a man can rule well his own home. I want to thank him for showing me that reading the Bible and praying are what men do. I want to thank him for understanding when I wanted to something other than be a farmer. Perhaps the best word that describes Wendell E. Blackstone and Joseph of Nazareth is "there." They were there when someone needed something. They were there at the meeting whether at the church or synagogue. He was there when grandchildren were born, and there when they celebrate their birthdays. He was there when someone new moves into town. He was there when a helping hand was needed. The purpose of his life was to be there. There to provide for, to pray for, and to prepare his children for their callings. As his oldest son, I know that if my father hadn't been there, I wouldn't be here. And I wonder if Jesus felt the same way about his earthly father Joseph.

A PEACE OVER NAZARETH

LUKE 2:14 GLORY TO God in the highest, and peace on earth, good will toward men.

If the Prince of Peace (Isaiah 9:6) brought peace to the earth at his birth, don't you believe that Nazareth was a peaceful place when he was a boy living there?

If I were asked to summarize my childhood in one word, it would have to be the word peaceful. Is there a rarer quality in this world today then peace? It is a virtue that has become more valuable than the desired diamond or the rarest ruby. It has become a prize sought by the most powerful and the most poor, yet they have not been able to attain unto it. It has become the pastime of the most skillful diplomats as well as the neighbor next door, yet despite all attempts to capture it peace has remained an elusive goal for most. When will mankind realize that true peace is only found in Christ? And to think the Nazarenes had that Peace with them for nearly thirty years!

The Perham, Maine, I knew in the 1950s and 1960s was a land at peace with itself and its inhabitants. I would even be so bold as to call it a place of perfect peace. Man and nature working and living hand in hand with each other. Oh, there was the occasional difference of opinion on the weather needed at a particular time, but the sun shone and the early and the latter rains came, and the crops grew and the cows matured, and springtime, summertime, harvest time and wintertime passed in unison one with the other. Year passed from year to year with no panic, only peace. Some might say I was living in a fantasy world unaffected by the problems that did exist, but Nazareth or no Nazareth, I knew my world was at peace. I knew peace when I felt it, faced it, and found it. I felt it in the loving relationship of my family. I faced it every day as I worked around the farm. I found it in the forest and fields of the farm and in the faces of my family and friends. And I believe so did Jesus.

In the 3530 plus years of recorded human history mankind has sought peace. According to the scholars only two hundred and eighty-six of those years have been years of peace. Why is that? The answer for me is simple. Man doesn't really want peace. There was peace on my family's homestead because there were people who really wanted peace and were ready, willing, and able to pay the price for peace. Perham became a peaceful place to practice peace. I recall very few fights, squabbles, or outbursts. I was brought up in a tolerant, calm, and relaxed environment and this despite cows dying, crops failing, and children aligning. So amid uncertain futures, unfulfilled dreams, and unpleasant circumstances, there is one piece of the farm that has stayed with me over these many years—peace, because it was in Perham that I too met Jesus Christ, the Prince of Peace and one of the gifts He left us, His peace (John 14:27).

A HOPE IN NAZARETH

EZRA 10:2 ... NOW there is hope in Israel ...

My ancestral home in Perham, Maine, much like Jesus' boyhood home in Nazareth, had withstood enormous challenges over the years. Despite the stress and strain of summer droughts and winter blizzards it remains. Despite the pressure and pounding of spring rains and falling snow it survived. With undaunted courage my forefathers, as did Jesus' ancestors, managed to keep stable a life and a lifestyle through seasons of illness, crop failure, financial reversals, domestic disappointments, and the death of a matriarch and patriarch or two. What was it that has kept alive the Blackstone dream and Israel's desire (I Samuel 9:20)? One irreplaceable ingredient—hope.

The homestead has rebounded against wind and weather, calamity and catastrophe, disease and death, and insects and isolation because of hope. It learned early in its existence that one can survive months without passable roads, weeks without rain, and days without the sun, but no house, home, homestead, or nation can last one moment without hope. Without hope you don't press on through a hot dry summer; without hope you throw in the towel when half your year's wages rot in the bin; and without hope you quit planting potatoes and when you stop planting, you stop harvesting and the farm stops. Hope is the irreducible catalyst of determination. Unless a life is anchored to hope there will be no joy of living and unless a land is bathed in hope there will be no happy harvest either, and unless a nation rests in the hope of a Messiah, they die.

Years later, the truth of Jesus coming from Galilee confused the religious leaders because they thought that out of Bethlehem would come the Messiah (John 7:52). Of course, they had missed Him at Bethlehem, so they were unaware that the hope of Israel had been living and abiding in

Nazareth for nearly thirty years. In some of my earliest remembrances of my family's farm the reoccurrence of the word hope comes to my memory. I never realized it then, but as I reflect on the bites and pieces of past conversations that still rattle around in my brain, I recall hearing "Hope it rains today; hope the wind comes up to dry the hay; hope the frost stays away for a few more days so we can finish digging; hope the vet finds out what's wrong with No. 68 (a cow); hope Lori (childhood diabetic) feels better." Now I see I lived in a refuge of hope, a place and a people who kept on hoping even when it didn't rain, the wind didn't blow, the frost came early, old 68 died, and Lori (my youngest sister) got worse.

Little did the citizens of Nazareth realize it, but they too were living with Hope. Little did they know that when they walked by Joseph's son, they were passing Hope. When they talked to Mary's son, they were talking to the Hope of their salvation and the Hope of the world.

THE SKY OVER NAZARETH

Job 37:18 Hast thou with Him spread out the sky . . .

Among the souvenirs I treasure in the scrapbook of my mind are the pictures of the sky over my family homestead in Perham, Maine. I believe that looking at the sky over Nazareth was also one of Jesus' favorite pastimes.

As in any place, Perham or Nazareth, there are four kinds of sky one sees each day, even on a potato and dairy farm in rural northern Maine and, yes, even in the foothills of Galilee. First, there is the day sky divided between morning and afternoon. On any given day it might be a gray sky filled with threatening storm clouds that will either deliver a much needed rain in the summer or a blanket of white in the winter. Or on any given day it might be a blue sky dotted with billowing white clouds or on some days only blue. In spring it is a dull blue reflecting the season just passed, but in autumn it is a bright blue, radiant and refreshing, preparing us for the season to come. As Jesus watched these different canvases unfold, did he remember the day He, one by one, spread them across the firmament He called heaven? (Genesis 1:8)

Second, there is the dusk sky that ushers in the night. How I use to love to set on the front porch of my boyhood home and watch the fire ball sink in the west. Depending on the day sky the sky at dusk could either reveal the glow of the sun slowly fading or the rays of the sun reflecting off the low hanging clouds. Each was spectacular to witness. How often did Jesus watch the setting sun? How is it I believe that Jesus took time to watch the changing sky? Remember later on when the people sought a sign, Jesus said, "When it is evening, ye say, it will be fair weather: for the sky is red. And in the morning, it will be foul weather today: for the sky is red and lowering." (Matthew 16:2, 3) Jesus was a sky watcher!

THE SKY OVER NAZARETH

Third, there is the dark sky. Most people go inside at the advent of night, but I have always been a night person. Some of the greatest shows I have ever observed have been provided by the dark sky. For those of you who haven't had the privilege of seeing a northern night sky, you will probably never understand my love of the glorious northern lights. As huge spotlights streaking up into the dark night, the arch of an Aurora Borealis is marvelous to see. Spanning the northern sky with its fiery columns, the night takes on an almost heavenly scene. Each time I see the splendor of that sight, I am reminded that its beacon is pointing home. Is that why Jesus looked skyward because skyward was homeward?

Fourth, there is the dawn sky. I have left the best for last. No doubt there is beauty in all the skies mentioned, but the dawn sky is the best. It is at dawn that you can see Venus and Mercury—the morning stars, the brightest stars. Jesus knew that one day he would be called by John "the bright and morning star" (Revelation 22:16), and He was.

SOLITUDE FROM NAZARETH

Isaiah 35:1 ... the solitary place shall be glad ...

We know that when Jesus became an adult that he loved to escape to a solitary place. (Mark 1:35) I believe he got his love of solitude from his time in Nazareth.

It is Friday again, and Friday means solitude for me. Some people take a day off, but for me I need only a day of solitude. For many people, a day alone is a day of loneliness. For others, solitary confinement is a form of punishment, but for me it is the best day of the week. Modern man recoils from the idea of being isolated, but I learned very early from my Savior that solitude is both a blessing and a necessity in public ministry.

I was not off the family farm very long before I learned the reason for the western world's disliked of solitude. The concentration of communities has given most people a false sense of togetherness, and that masses and metropolitans are where it's at. Closeness has become important even though most don't even know their next door neighbor of a few feet away. We have convinced ourselves that being surrounded with others will solve all our problems. Yet in the statistical world we live in, we have discovered that these ant hills we call cities have only corrupted us more, not corrected our internal problems. We are teaching generations that to be alone is alienation, and alienation is failure. To be caught alone triggers thoughts in others of problems instead of peace. The peculiar paradox of this phobia is that those who are least alone are the loneliest, and those most alone are the least lonely.

When my father would send me out to the back forty to rack hay, I might be alone all morning. But I learned I would often get more work done alone then I would if I were laboring with my cousins. I have found this true in my adult life as well. For me, people have always been a distraction.

SOLITUDE FROM NAZARETH

My mind is clearest and sharpest when I am in solitude. It was during those solitude sessions in my boyhood sanctuary I really developed the five senses I was born with. Who can see clearly in a city? If the smog or skyscraper doesn't block your vision, then society will. Who can hear clearly in a city? If the telephone or television doesn't confuse your hearing, then other technologies will. Who can smell clearly in a city? If pollution or petrol doesn't destroy your ability to smell, then perfumes will. Who can taste clearly in a city? If additives or addictions don't control your tongue, then aspirin will. Who can touch clearly in a city? If artificial or synthetic doesn't trick you, then manmade will. When was the last time you used your senses?

Jesus developed his human senses while living in Nazareth. He learned early I believe that if he was to finish his mission then he would have to find times of solitude when only his Father was around. And he did.

A CRAFTSMAN IN NAZARETH

Mark 6:3 is not this the carpenter?

I can't imagine Jesus not being skillful with his hands. If Jesus lived in Nazareth for nearly thirty years, what did he do? Most believe Jesus became a carpenter (years later he was call "the carpenter"). Did the boy Jesus work hand in hand with Joseph? Probably. Did the young man Jesus take over the family business when his father died? Maybe. The Creator of all must have been a fantastic craftsman in wood. As for me, I tell people all the time that my hands are the least crafty members of my body, but I do know a craftsman with an exceptional talent for carpentry.

There aren't many master craftsmen left on this planet. Men who work with their hands are few and far between. Being an amateur historian, I have read a lot about the development of hand skills. The Egyptians were probably the first great craftsmen testified by the great pyramids and tombs of their pharaohs which are still a puzzle to man today. Just how did they do that? Add to them the Greeks and a Michelangelo or two, and you will conclude as I have that such men are rare. Men and women who can fashion works of art out of stone, bronze, gold, silver or wood are to be commended and acknowledged for their skill.

Hidden away in an oat bin in the huge cow barn on the homestead is a woodsman's workshop. Little did anyone in the family know of my brother's talents until after Jay married Tami Sue? Then Christmas after Christmas Jay began to make furniture for Christmas presents, and we began to discover what was being created in that old oat bin. They were simple things at first. The first JB original we received was a short book stand. It is still in my son's old room. It held his baseball and basketball card collections. One year Jay built my wife an antique- looking pitcher and towel stand that sets proudly today in our dining room. My pride and joy is a clock fashioned in the shape of the state of Maine made out of Blackstone pine. Instead of numbers Jay put Atlantic Salmon Flies, and it hangs in my study today. Then one Christmas Jay crafted for my entire family an oak television and VCR cabinet. We haven't been the only recipients of Jay's handiwork. A few years back Jay built an elaborate cabinet in which my sister-in-law Julie could store her piano music. The twelve drawers Blackstone ash cabinet with brass handles drew a lot of oohs and has from the family gathered around. I remember the year Jay presented to his wife a full length oval oak floor mirror. You talk about something elegant! Then there is his daughter's bed, Jay's latest masterpiece, specially handcrafted so that it can meet her sleeping needs until she is in a normal bed. It contains two huge drawers underneath for all her frilly dresses. Jay Blackstone, the craftsman from Perham.

    I wonder what Jesus made with his skilled hands?

DEW ON NAZARETH

Psalms 133:3 as the dew of Hermon . . .

When Jesus made (John 1:3) the first irrigation system for this planet ("a mist from the earth, and watered the whole face of the ground" (Genesis 2:6), He created the dew also. The Jewish historian, Josephus, described Nazareth this way in his classic work. "The land is everywhere so rich in soil and pasturage and produces such variety of trees, that even the most indolent are tempted . . . to devote themselves to agriculture. In fact, every inch of the soil has been cultivated by the inhabitants." When the Psalmist speaks of the dew of Hermon, Jesus himself not only could see Mount Hermon from Nazareth, but he also experienced the morning dew that helped water the fields and vineyards.

Being the firstborn son of a farmer and having been raised on a farm, I know about dew. Often I remember my dad speaking of the blessings of the dew. In a dry Maine summer the dew was sometimes the only moisture the potato plants and the oat stalks would get for weeks on end. The late summer dew supplemented the absence of the latter rains. Heavy morning dew would often fool you into thinking that it had showered overnight. Walking through the pasture and herding the Holsteins to the milking shed would result in your overalls getting soaked clean through. "Rouging" (a county word for weeding) in the early morning through waist-high potato rows was just like wading through Beaver Brook by the time you got to the end of the field. I have at times had to stop mowing my grandfather's lawn because the dew was so heavy the grass would clog the mower. Have you ever picked an apple right off the tree still dripping with dew? I have many times, and there is nothing more delicious and desirable to eat.

Dew is a silent shower without thunder or lighting to announce it. It quietly forms in the darkness of the night to water the earth in the brightness of the day. Unseen and unheard, it cools the air and covers the land, refreshing and reviving each and every homestead and homesteader. Father often spoke of how the dew not only watered but fertilized the fields. As a mid-summer drought took hold and the potato plants languished under the intense heat, their appearance was sad to observe. We might go to bed thinking they could not survive another day under a scorching sun, and then almost miraculously by the next morning they were growing and glowing. The dew had fallen, and the crop was saved. The fruitfulness of the farm could be at least in part contributed to the reclusive rain called dew.

More often than not the dew of the earth is created on a clear, calm night. This invisible irrigation was probably responsible for more bumper crops than any other factor, yet it hasn't gotten the recognition it justly deserves. So, three cheers for the dew of the dales and the Citizen of Nazareth who formed it by His divine hand.

THE MOON OVER NAZARETH

PSALMS 104:19 HE APPOINTED the moon for seasons...

Jesus' days in Nazareth were no doubt filled with the common activities of a small marketplace town. The hub of Nazareth was no doubt the street shops and the craftsmen who made and sold their wares, one of them being Jesus' earthly dad, the carpenter Joseph. When evening would come as with most small towns, the citizens returned to their homes and waited out the night. One of the great symbols of night is the full moon. How did Jesus react from an earthly standpoint to the "light He created to rule the night?" (Genesis 1:16)

I have had over the years favorite full moons. One of the best was the full moon for the month of April, 1994. It shone brightest on the twenty-fourth and twenty-fifth days of that month. I drove to my father-in-law's home in its glare through a foggy northern Maine Sunday night. When I saw it again the next night, I was sitting on the porch of Vicker's Camp on the banks of the mighty Miramichi River. Both encounters with this "lesser light that rules the night" sparked remembrances from my childhood when the full moon would rise over my beloved homestead in Perham, Maine.

I recalled the evenings that same moon would shine down on my winter wonderland. Peeking out from behind a cloud bank, its rays would turn the whole countryside around my folks' house into a ghostly gray. As the clouds parted and the moonshine was unobstructed, the light reflecting off the white snow turned heavenly. I can still see in my mind's eye that I felt safe in the glow of that brilliant moon as I looked out my second story bedroom window.

I recalled the evenings that same moon would shine down on a summer evening while sitting on the porch. Rover, my dog, would be relaxing in his favorite corner as the moon made its way up from behind the eastern hills toward Caribou. Dad would come out for a moment of fresh air before heading off to bed as the moon shone through the hardwood ridge that overshadowed our old farmhouse. Sylvia, my sister, would be reading as the moon crested the tops of the trees. Mum would come out and say it was time for bed just as the full moon took command of the night sky. I am sixty-seven years old and how many full moons I have seen I know not, but last week I stood and stared again as if it were the first time. Just as I did the first night, I watched one of God's great creations make a curtain call over my homestead. Did Jesus do the same thing when His masterpiece of night came up behind the hills to the east of Nazareth?

What must it have been like for the Creator God to view the glory of a full harvest moon knowing what He knew about it versus what everybody else knew? It took mankind hundreds of years to discover its makeup, and 1969 years to go there. As each season passed in Nazareth, did Jesus use the moon to keep track of how much longer he would stay in Nazareth?

A MOONSET OVER NAZARETH

PSALMS 89:37 IT SHALL be established forever as the moon, and as a faithful witness in heaven.

One of the great things about living on this planet is that the same moonset I saw in Ellsworth (where I now live) this morning is the same moonset Jesus watched thousands of years ago in Nazareth. I also watched just a few years ago the only annular eclipse I will ever witness in the skies over Maine. Not since 1875 in the northeast had the moon passed before the sun as it did that Tuesday. The full moon surrounded by a blazing ring in mid-afternoon was a sight to behold as is every moonset of "a faithful witness."

It was one of those clear, chilly nights. A full moon aglow in milky white rose steadily into a star-studded spring sky. A typical country day in Nazareth was coming to a close. The marketplace was settling down to a much needed rest. Hour by hour the moon rose higher and higher from the eastern horizon. Soon every hill and hollow, field and forest in Nazareth was shining with a bright mantle of light. A lonely moo could be heard from the pasture behind Joseph's carpenter shop. A dark ghostly shadow could be seen crossing the lane as the neighborhood dog made his way home from an afternoon excursion to somewhere. The final cock-a-doodle doos could be heard from the chickens that ran wild around the town square as the round ball of white escaped the tree line. The evening breeze subsided as the boy Jesus made his way home from a productive day helping his earthly father. Was it then he thought of His heavenly Father and His business?

W. Phillip Keller once wrote, **"All the world waited for morning, but before dawn came, the moon must set."** Jesus heard Joseph up first as he sleepily got out of bed. His job was to get water from the local spring before he headed for the carpenter shop. As Jesus made his way out through the back door, he noticed the moon through the window slowly, steadily, and surely sinking behind the low hills to the west of Nazareth. The white light of night had turned into a golden glow reflecting the morning sun to the east. Stepping into the backyard, the setting moon spread its final glow over the landscape. As Jesus lowered the clay pitcher into the well, he took one last glace at the morning moonset. Its final few moments of glory captured his attention as they have touched my imagination and inspiration. Only those who have witnessed the ending of the dark and the beginning of the dawn know of the breathless beauty of a moonset, **"the mystery and the majesty of the moment"** says Keller.

How can such a moment last these many years? Buried deep in time that moonset has survived while countless other events have become lost in time. Could the answer be in the simplicity of the occasion? A morning moonset is only as good and glorious and grand as a spring sunrise in Nazareth.

A CONCERT NEAR NAZARETH

ECCLESIASTES 12:4 . . . AND He shall rise up at the voice of the bird . . .

I have come to believe that Jesus was a bird watcher because he often used birds in His illustrations (Matthew 6:26 and Matthew 10:29). When springtime came to Nazareth was Jesus found at times listening to a country concert?

Have you ever taken the time to listen to a rural recital? I have many times. I have stood alone beside a stretch of forest in an empty field on the backside of the farm. A faint breeze blowing through the deep woods calls the songbirds to rehearsal. It is a perfect setting as a feathered flutist begins the concert. There is something heavenly about such moments; the hallowed hollows shush into quietness at its first note. Added to the freshness of spring, the sweet sound fills your soul with such tranquility that you wonder if you have been transported to a celestial place. Did Jesus feel that way as he remembered each and every sound He put into the throat of the various birds that called Nazareth home?

Nearby a woodpecker pounds out a beat which only adds to the music of the songbird. High up in the sky, the honking of a passing flight of wild geese heading home adds a deep bass sound to the chorus. To my left, a low, sad whoo-oo, hoo, hoo, hoo of a duet of mourning doves creates a solemnity to the music. Soon the caw, caw, caw of a trio of crows interrupt the melody, but as I listen, their harsh sounds blend with the music being played. In a world where harmony is almost extinct, it is nice to be able to go to a place where creatures still can live and sing in harmony. We could learn much from a country choir because behind all such concerts is the Master Conductor. Did Jesus lead such gatherings in his boyhood town of Nazareth?

A CONCERT NEAR NAZARETH

The tree swallow is at it again as if to take back the solo he began, but he cannot. He has begun something that has taken on a life of its own. It seems as if that one swallow has started the whole of creation singing. Rover (my childhood dog), my companion for the day, begins to howl against the noises of the forest. The Holstein herd in the pasture across the field reacting to Rover's bark begins their deep mooing, perhaps because they think something is wrong. Caught up in the music of the meadow, this country conductor starts to wave his arms as if leading nature's grandest orchestra. There are no words to this musical piece and no music score, but the sound is a song heard often in my barnyard boyhood. I faintly hear it even in the city. Did Jesus miss these special concerts when he moved to the bigger cities of Galilee?

I do not know how Jesus reacted to the songbirds of Nazareth, but I know this. The Creator of these singers understood clearly their melody and the message. (Psalms 148:10)

A RAIN IN NAZARETH

Psalms 147:8 who covereth the heaven with clouds who prepareth rain for the earth . . .

Have you ever wondered as a storm would gather over the ridge that was Nazareth that the boy Jesus would have said to himself, "I made the clouds, I created the rain?" Do you think he watched the falling rain as a well-known artist stepping back to admire his latest masterpiece? The weatherman says it's going to rain. I like when the rain falls. I learned on the family farm just how precious the rain would have been to a farming community like Nazareth.

The refreshing rain was always welcome in Perham, Maine, except perhaps during haying season. Its benefits were always greater than its liabilities, particularly if it was a gentle overnight rain. Driving downpours were disastrous, but a soft summer shower was ideal. My memory still recalls the sound of pitter/patter, pitter/patter, pitter/patter on the roof in the evening just after going to bed. The small raindrops would wash the windows in my bedroom, but more importantly they were soaking the sod with life-giving moisture. I would fall sleep with the satisfaction that God was giving His creation a good drink.

The next morning after the rain clouds had passed, the grass seemed greener, the leaves on the trees seemed fuller, and the flowers around the farm house seemed to be more beautiful. If the rain came after a short drought, the potato plants would spring back to life overnight, the oats would head out, and the clover would smell sweeter. Everything that had been dusty before would have been washed clean. The air smelled fresher, and the land looked spotless. The dryness of days past had been exchanged with restoration and rejuvenation.

A RAIN IN NAZARETH

Everybody on the homestead felt the renewal only a rain could bring. I have watched the Holstein herd bathe unaffected in the middle of the pasture under a spring shower. I have witnessed my dog Rover barking for joy in the midst of an August downpour after a long hot summer with little rain. I have worked through a rain to get a field picked clean of rocks, ready for planting. The rain cooled the air and the task. There is something about timely rain.

A country cloudburst, a summer shower, a day-long drizzle, or a drenching downpour are some of the ways a rural rain might come. Each contained the one ingredient that makes the country the country, water. Precipitation or condensation, call it what you will. Rainstorm or thunderstorm, call it as you see it. From sprinkles to showers, from dizzily to drippy, rain is the only cure I know for drought or dryness in the city or in the country. Jesus also knew of these things, but he had an advantage that the rest of us don't have: He knew when because He was the one that "covereth the heaven with clouds" and "prepareth rain for the earth" every time it rained in Nazareth or Perham.

A REFLECTION ABOUT NAZARETH

MARK 1:9 AND IT came to pass in those days that Jesus came from Nazareth of Galilee . . .

Looking back over the years, I have often reflected on the blessing of being raised in a barnyard instead of on a boulevard. I am thankful for being reared in the country instead of the city. Vance Havner once wrote, "God made the country and manmade the town, and you certainly can see the difference!" I have wondered at times if Jesus had similar reflections on his country versus city upbringing.

I am grateful for memories of potato fields and cow pastures, for maple trees in the front yard and spruce trees in the backyard, for swallows in the barn and chickens in the barnyard. I can still see the American crow soaring in the evening sky being chased by sparrows. I can still hear the crickets in the fields and bull frogs in the pond across the road. What a wonderful privilege I had to taste the homestead life before progress modernized the farm.

I am thankful that I was trained to be a "man for all seasons." I type today on the threshold of another change of seasons. Within weeks, spring will come. Though I have my favorites, each of the four seasons were special in northern Maine. I loved the white world of winter, the sweet sounds of spring, the sunny scenes of summer, and the full foliage of fall. Winter was the silent season that kept me in and made me thankful that God didn't create just one season. Spring was the season of rebirth and resurrection that reminded me that no matter how tough and rough life could be that there was always a spring ahead. Summer was like the song ways, "the good old summertime." It recharged my body as well as my spirit. Autumn was

A REFLECTION ABOUT NAZARETH

the season that could have a bit of all the other seasons in it, from falling leaves to falling snow, from spring-like temperatures to summer-like temperatures. A new season is upon me, but the memories of past seasons still fill my mind with fond remembrances.

As I reflect on these blessings, I realize I owe much to the time in which I was born. In my youth, I complained of God's timing, but as I near seventy I am thankful I was honored to have been not only a part of a family farm, but a Maine homestead. So if I have any advice to those who might be travelling the road behind me, it would be this. Take the time to enjoy "Another Day in Nazareth." The seasons wax and wane so quickly that unless you stop to watch the seasons change, you will miss most of life. The seasons pass with their songs and savor and unless you take the time to learn their melodies and experiences their taste, you might miss out on what life is all about. Spring is upon me, but I will blink tomorrow and it will be summer. One breath after that and it will be fall. Autumn will huff and puff for a few moments and will blow into winter and before I know it, I will be standing where I am today, but it will be a year later.

A STORM OVER NAZARETH

Isaiah 6:4 . . . from storm and from rain.

As summer moved slowly into August, the heat and humidity intensified in Nazareth. All the surrounding lands, colored in grass greened by the spring showers of May and June, were gone. The searing sun of July had turned the area brown as nature died of thirst. Shade less soil cried for rain. The "dog days" of summer had arrived in Jesus' boyhood home, and he prayed for a storm.

Sometimes, the first sign that a storm was on the way was a silent stillness. Suddenly the dry, hot air would stop blowing through the trees already hanging limp from lack of water. The song birds stopped singing as they too sought shade against the steadily rising temperatures. Even the normal farm work and town work was suspended. It was just too hot to work outside. All eyes of the citizens of Nazareth lifted skyward in hopes that the clouds building in the western sky over the Mediterranean Sea were filled with water.

As the billowing black clouds moved into the area and blocked out the sun, a bright, colorful streak of light exploded over the ridge. Thunder followed rumbling through the hollows and tumbling over the hills. Again and again the lightning crashed over the fields and the town was aglow with celestial light. With each ignition thunder shook the ground where Jesus stood. With the coming of the clouds, the wind once again blew heavily announcing the approach of a storm. How often did Jesus watch a storm's creation from the door of the carpenter shop? Each time did he stand in wonder at the grandeur of a summer storm that He had made of stillness, sound, and sheets of fire?

As far as his eye could see, the storm clouds had taken over the area. What was always amazing was that just a few hours earlier the sky had been

A STORM OVER NAZARETH

an August blue without a cloud to be seen. Now the darkness, comparable to a moon-lit night, was only illuminated by the electrical energy sweeping the landscape periodically. Despite the awesome show of power, Nazareth was still dusty and drab. Minute upon minute passed as the thunder and lighting and wind dominated the village, but amid the numbing noise another sound began to vibrate through the streets. At first, it was only a gentle tapping, but in time it built to a heavy pounding. After a long, hot drought, rain on the roof and over the ridge was a stirring, satisfying sound.

Raindrops began to fall at Jesus' feet as he stepped back into the shop. He could hear the tiny water droplets hitting the ground as the heavens opened up and the rain clouds began to drench the thirsty topsoil. Cloudburst after cloudburst poured on Nazareth until the streets could take no more. And as fast as it blew in, it blew over. The clouds soon left, the sun came out, and along with it, a new world. A summer storm had worked its magic in Nazareth.

A SUCCOURER IN NAZARETH

PROVERBS 11:16 A GRACIOUS woman retaineth honour . . .

    Lois thought she never accomplished much in Nazareth.
    Lois was always a very busy woman. Lois' husband had died leaving her with over thirty years of living alone. Lois use to complain to the boy Jesus that she hadn't done much for Jehovah during her life. Her early days, after her husband Reuben's death, were spent in a candle shop located next to Joseph's carpenter shop trying to make ends meet. Her six children had all married by this time, but that didn't make life any easier for Lois. Even when she had retired to live her old age out on the other side of town with one of her daughters, her fervent spirit for work kept her busy right up to her final days. There was food to prepare for that sick neighbor in need. There were clothes to fix and make for the synagogue kids. There were bandages to wrap for the lepers who lived outside of Nazareth. There were flowers that had to be planted and tended so there would be a bouquet for a family member or a friend that got ill or at the synagogue on the Sabbath. There were visits to be made to her neighbors and family scattered throughout Nazareth, especially to the son of Joseph and Mary whom she loved as her own. Lois did all these things not for reward or to be over-religious, but because she loved Jehovah and them.
    One day Lois fell sick, and the shadow of death gathered around her frail body. As in life she struggled for life, but after a long fight she passed into glory. As she began to walk along the streets of gold, she met a young man that looked very familiar. Something so strangely dark on earth became crystal clear in heaven. Lois apologized for not recognizing Jesus during her earthly pilgrimage in Nazareth complaining she just seemed to have been too busy. Jesus replied, "What are you talking about?" "Oh you know," explained Lois, "my never having enough time for you." "For me?"

exclaimed the Lord. "Why you always had time for me." "I did?" asked Lois. "When?" Then Jesus said, "You mean you don't remember all those meals you cooked for me when I was sick, or those colorful clothes you use to make for me each winter so I wouldn't get cold? Or those bandages you wrapped to cover my sores, or the flowers you grew so my house would be beautiful on the Sabbath? And what about those countless times you talked to me? What do you mean you never had time for me? You gave all your time for me in Nazareth!"

It was then that Lois finally remembered the words of Jesus that He had said to her on their walks home after work that she never understood. "Verily I say unto you, inasmuch as ye have done it unto one of the least of these my brethren, ye have done it unto me." (Matthew 25:40) Lois' life would become one of the cornerstone doctrines of Jesus' teaching when he became the preacher from Galilee.

THE CREED OF NAZARETH

Luke 4:16 He came to Nazareth where He had been brought up.

I have a simple country creed, a terrain theology, a farm faith. Years ago, in my barnyard boyhood, I decided to stake all that I am or ever hope to be on the teachings of a country carpenter from Nazareth. Though I left the Blackstone homestead in Perham, Maine, nearly fifty years ago, I still live in the fragrance and faith of Nazareth.

When Jesus strolled the back lanes of Judea, he taught through trees and birds and seeds. Perhaps this is why I picked up his theology so quickly in my youth. The more I read of his philosophy the more I could relate to it through my surroundings on the homestead. When he talked of the sower going forth to sow his seeds, I could see my grandfather and father doing the very same thing. When he spoke of the sparrow and its fall, I too watched as the little bird tumbled from the hayloft to the barn floor. When he spoke of the trees and their significance to the kingdom, I understood the meaning of the forest because I lived by one. I still don't understand everything the Man from Galilee was saying, but I do understand his object lessons from Nazareth because they were much like my days of walking in the hills and living in the hollows of Perham.

In the complexity of sunlight and shadows I saw in the darkness during a walk through the cow barn just how black sin can be in the human heart, but I also discovered in the light of midday, homestead sun, just how brilliant the glory of the Lord can be. As I grew, the farmyard fables of sheep and shepherds became to me the same as herds of Holsteins and herdsmen. Sheep were replaced by cows. When "green pastures" and "still waters" were mentioned, my mind's eye immediately viewed the Russell Place with its ponds and creeks in pasture land of green fields. The longer I live the more

THE CREED OF NAZARETH

I am convinced that my real seminary training began long before I went off to Bible school in South Carolina.

In my childhood, I spent most of my free days outdoors. Whether working in the fields or playing in the forests, I was contently faced with reality. Life and death were a normal part of life. Long before I faced my first funeral, I had looked death in the eye and learned it was nothing to fear or be afraid of. Whether a feline or a friend, death was just part of life and living. I also learned that the simple pleasures of life were much more rewarding then the worldly pleasures of sin. To pick dandelions in the spring and to listen to song birds in the summer were much more pleasurable then picking up friends and going to the movies. A walk along the fence line was far more joyful then a walk through the red light district. I have come to the city to minister, but my creed is still well established in the lessons from Galilee and the teaching of Nazareth. I preach today an outdoors kind of faith to an indoors kind of world!

THE COMMUNITY OF NAZARETH

LUKE 4:34 . . . SAYING, Let us alone; what have we to do with thee. Thou Jesus of Nazareth . . .

I was a farmer's son. I lived in a hollow about three miles from the small hamlet of Perham, Maine. Perham consisted of a number of small homes, a few potato houses along the railroad tracks that ran through town, a general store, an elementary school, and a Baptist church. This community was nestled in the northern region of the potato-producing county of Aroostook. Jesus was a carpenter's son. He lived on a hill about fifteen miles from the Sea of Galilee and the big city of Capernaum. Nazareth was a crossroad town with an interesting population and community, like Perham.

The Perham I remember was a country community where everybody kept to themselves except when there was a great need or it was Sunday. The community didn't have much time to socialize because there was a lot of work to do. Perham was a farming community through and through. Everybody either had their own farm or they worked for somebody who did. I remember my grandfather speaking of a time when Perham was known more for its wood industry, but I only remember farming. By the time I arrived in Perham in 1951 the shingle mill was gone as well as most of the woods operations. Oh, there was always a few cutting a little fire wood or some pulp wood, but Perham in the 1950s and 1960s was strictly agriculture-based as was Nazareth.

The people of the lower Galilee were made up of both Jews and Gentiles. The Syrians were there having moved down from the north to the fertile lands around the Sea of Galilee. The Greeks had moved in after the

THE COMMUNITY OF NAZARETH

conquests of Alexander the Great, and the Romans arrived about a hundred years before the birth of Jesus. Jesus would have mingled with these different people groups, but the community where he was raised would have been pure Hebrew, a community where helping and helpfulness was a way of life.

I still recall the times after we finished harvesting our crop of potatoes on the homestead that Dad would take the digger and a barrel truck and head down the road to help a neighbor finish digging. More often than not the neighbor would be a relative. A lot of family lived and farmed in Perham in those days. The village of Perham was a small closed community in my day. Most of what we wanted out of life was found in Perham as with Nazareth. Few trips were made to Washburn, Caribou or Presque Isle (Chorazin, Bethsaida, and Capernaum) in those days because our community supplied our every need. Today all of the farmers are gone. You can't buy a loaf of bread or a gallon of gas. Perham is now a suburb not a community. I wonder if Jesus saw the same thing happen in his community as the Hellenistic culture began to change the village of Nazareth.

SLEEPING IN NAZARETH

PSALMS 121:4 BEHOLD, HE that keepeth Israel shall neither slumber nor sleep.

Can you imagine what it was like for the Son of God to sleep? When you're raised on a hard working farm, sleep was an important part of your life. To endure the tasks of an active dairy and potato homestead, rest was essential as you worked from sunrise to sunset. I learned very early in life that to enjoy work, a good sleep was just what the doctor ordered. The boy Jesus also experienced the value of a good night's rest, and, yes, maybe a good afternoon nap as he changed from a sleepless existence to a human necessity.

I learned how to sleep from the master, my dad, Wendell E. Blackstone. Dad could and still can sleep anywhere. I have pictures of Dad sleeping with his head propped against a boulder which was located along the shoreline of a river in northern Quebec during a fishing trip together. I can still see in my mind's eye dad resting against a tire of his Model G John Deere tractor during a noontime nap in a potato field. Dad's favorite place to rest was our old couch in the corner of the living room. After a hearty lunch, Dad could be asleep within seconds of laying his head down. Though I never perfected the amazing speed by which Dad could get to sleep, I too had my favorite places to sleep in Perham. Did Jesus have such places in Nazareth?

The first I recall was the stoop in the bay window that was located in the dining room of my childhood home. The huge window, especially large when you're just a little lad, opened up to the backyard barnyard. Sunday afternoons at the Blackstone house was for eating, that is until it was time to milk the cows. After the biggest meal of the week, it was nice to curl up in that sunny spot and it seemed to only take minutes to drop off to sleep. The combination of a full stomach and the warm rays of the sun are still the best

SLEEPING IN NAZARETH

sleeping pill in the world. I always hated to hear Dad's call to chores when I was sleeping in that bay window. Where were Jesus' sunny places to sleep?

The next place I remember for its sleep was our cow barn. Many times of rest I had nestled between two bales of straw using my jacket as a pillow. Naps could be taken when I waited for the next load of hay to come from the field. Another time of rest was during lunch hour. Instead of returning home for a meal, many times Mum would bring our meals to us especially during the busy time of haying. A quick nap would provide the energy to finish piling that last load of hay for the day. Did Jesus have such a spot in the carpenter's shop of Nazareth?

Sleep is something many today don't seem to get much of. Perhaps the reason is they never learned the joy of resting wherever they were. A comfortable spot in a sunny or shady place is all that is required for a good sleep.

DOWNTOWN IN NAZARETH

LUKE 1:26 ... UNTO a city in Galilee, named Nazareth.

Despite living in the country, Jesus would have experienced the activities of downtown. In those days the hub of a typical hamlet such as Nazareth would have been a collection of homes around a central street where the local craftsmen (like Joseph) would have made and sold their wares. The carpenter would have been near the smith because their combined skills would have been necessary to make and repair the farming equipment (iron-tipped plows, sickles, cart wheels, wagons) needed in the outlying fields. There would have been basket weavers, candle makers, and potters along this street as well. Jesus knew of downtown, and so do I because Perham had its own hub of streets and buildings.

Just last week Dad, Mum, and I were talking about the village of Perham when I was a lad. Today, there are only a few homes. The potato houses are gone. The stores are gone. The railroad tracks are gone. The school is gone. The gas pumps are gone. Downtown Perham is no more the Norman Rockwell painting of my past. Time had a slow pace when I was a kid growing up in Perham. My year was eight months of school plus two months of summer vacation plus a month of school plus a month of potato harvest. My world was Perham with the occasional trip to the really big cities of Presque Isle or Caribou or the town of Washburn. Everything we wanted we could get in Perham. What couldn't be bought in Perham was ordered from the Sears and Roebuck catalog. Both Dad and Mum had strong feelings about patronizing the local merchants. They were neighbors and friends and people you went to church with on Sunday. Of course, K-Mart and Wal-Mart hadn't been invented yet, and why should they when you had Holts General Store—the hub of downtown Perham. The store was a two-story building in the middle of the village. A little bit of everything could be found, purchased, and heard there. Across the street, actually the Perham/Washburn Road was the only church building in town. It was the local sanctuary and the assembly hall for the eight grade-four room Perham Elementary School. How many people do you know can say they were married in the same room they graduated from elementary school? And when everyone showed up for Sunday services, there wasn't enough room to park all the cars in the small parking lot so they parked along both sides of the road. I pastor in a city now, and it is against the law to park on both sides of the streets around Emmanuel Baptist Church. Our neighbor gets very upset when we park on her lawn. In downtown Perham we had no such laws or neighbors. I wonder about Nazareth?

Downtown was not only the heart of Perham and Nazareth, it was also where people got together to work and to worship. I wonder, did Jesus have such fond memories of his experiences in downtown Nazareth?

A SIMPLICITY TO NAZARETH

II Samuel 15:11 ... they went in their simplicity ...

My homestead town was never simpler then during my boyhood years. Nearly forty year after that era, I believe I have come to an understanding why there was such simplicity. I also believe Jesus experienced a similar simplicity in Nazareth during his boyhood.

Life was simple then. The world was beginning to experience complications, but it didn't affect Perham, Maine, until the 1970s. I had nearly twenty years of simplicity that I have never experienced since. I discover every time I reflect back on my past that it doesn't take much money to enjoy life. It doesn't take a lot of things to really live. Now in the rat race to keep up with Hollywood and Madison Avenue, we have lost that simple simplicity I once knew back in Perham. The simplicity of a four-room, eight-grade schoolhouse instead of a multi-floor complex of gadgets and gangs. The simplicity of a sled instead of a snowmobile. The simplicity of a one channel television instead of a 360-channel satellite dish. The simplicity of an evening playing dominos instead of an evening fighting over which video tape to watch. The simplicity of barn chores instead of boredom. The simplicity of homemade instead of store bought. The simplicity of loving parents instead of divorced partners. The simplicity of math and English instead of computers and group encounter playacting. The simplicity of country lanes instead of traffic intersections. The simplicity of sunsets instead of street lights. The simplicity of neighborhood friends instead of turf wars. The simplicity of farm-grown vegetables instead of chemically altered produce.

Years ago we didn't have fancy, store-bought presents or gifts, food or clothes. We accepted a simple pair of sneakers that our parents didn't have to get a loan to purchase. Mother would make a large bowl of popcorn for my sister and me either on the stove or in the fireplace. It was slower to be sure (that age could never compete against the speed of this age), but the popcorn was better. The homemade bread was better, too. It was simple and beneficial as were the chocolate cakes and apples pies. Dad would help me make a toy or two, simple objects that filled our idle time with fun things to do with my neighbors or cousins. I believe the simple toys of my boyhood lasted longer than the modern creations that are so real. My childhood guns were crude, and it took a lot of imagination to play Cops and Robbers or Cowboys and Indians, but I don't remember any of my class mates being accidentally shot by a policeman because he thought we were playing with a real gun.

Simplicity is what this modern age is claiming to be about, but I ask this simple question, **"If life is so much more simpler now, why are things so complicated?"** I believe Jesus enjoyed the simplicity of Nazareth as I enjoyed the simplicity of Perham.

A RAINBOW OVER NAZARETH

REVELATION 4:3 . . . AND there was a rainbow round about . . .

J. J. Smith once wrote, "Rainbows are God's way of making up for those cloudy days in our lives." I don't remember many cloudy days in Perham, but I do recall my fair share of rainbows. Did Jesus love rainbows over Nazareth?

If my mind is any barometer (it has been known to be off), probably the first rainbow I ever saw was over my homestead in Perham, Maine. I can be pretty sure of that because I hardly left the farm of my birth for the first eighteen years of my life. At the time of my first sighting, I knew more of the Biblical source of rainbows then the scientific explanation. Prisms, refraction, and reflection came later in science class, but my first rainbow was seen as a promise fulfilled, that God would never again destroy the world by flood. I never even knew of the fabled pot of gold at the end of a rainbow before I began to mingle with the world. A rainbow in all of its arcs of color was a sign of our family's belief in the Creator God. And to think that the Creator of the rainbow got a chance to witness one of the masterpieces of His creation from a hillside in Galilee.

No doubt that first rainbow came in the summer after a brief shower. I will not try to remember the place or the position of that ribbon of dazzling lights, but I will recall that it touched my heart and not my head. I can see in my mind's eye the clouds dividing over the hills towards Caribou, and the sun's reappearance brought with it the wondrous beauty of the "bow." Transfixed by its colors and highlighted by the dark clouds near it, I became a rainbow watcher from that day on. The special rainbows that do remain in my memory are these. Standing in the entrance of the huge cow barn on the main homestead, I can still clearly see heaven's colorful spray arching over the forest between the farm and Perham village. We had just gotten a fresh load of clover under cover when the shower hit. The rain pounding on the barn roof lasted about ten minutes and then the sun suddenly reappeared and the rainbow could be seen from side to side of our heaven. I also recall a special rainbow that came to call after an exceptionally warm September rain. The fall potato harvest was in full swing, but the water drove everyone under cover. We were digging on the hill overlooking the Paul place, a wonderful vantage point to watch the appearance of a rainbow. What made these sights so spectacular was the combination of the fall foliage at its peak. Imagine if you will the brilliant color of the trees blending with the bright colors of the rainbow. At the rainbow's end, it seemed as if the surrounding forest had fused the two together.

Vivid rainbows formed quite often over my childhood homestead as they did in Nazareth. I no doubt missed a few "bows," but I still live in "the promise of the rainbow!"

SISTERS IN NAZARETH

MATTHEW 13:56 AND HIS sisters, are they not all with us?

I was blessed to have been brought up in a family in which I had two brothers and two sisters. I love them all dearly, but for the bulk of my childhood on the family homestead in northern Maine I only had one sister. This was because my parents were blessed with two families. My older sister Sylvia and I came along within ten months of each other in the first two years of the 1950s. My younger sister and my two younger brothers came along within the first five years of the 1960s. Sisters were something else I found in common with Jesus and his years in Nazareth.

Being the older sister, Sylvia was always there leading. I remember her in Children's Church when I took my first steps in worship. I remember her in elementary school when I took my first steps in education. I remember her in high school when I took my first steps out of my community. I remember her in collage when I took my first steps out-of-state. For the first twenty years of my life Sylvia pioneered the trail before me. Sylvia always went first, and the path seemed a bit easier knowing that she had already travelled it. Despite what people see in me now, I wasn't an outward, confident kid. My accomplishments as a child were only because my sister was there leading the way. I ponder, knowing what I know of Jesus, if he was the one leading his sisters through the early years in Nazareth.

Being the younger sister, Lori was often my charge. To say my sister Lori and I were close would be an understatement. I remember her entrance into our family as being a surprise to say the least, but a joyful surprise. After a decade, my first big revelation was that I would no longer be the youngest child. It was then I took the lead of my older sister and became a helper to this frail little lady. Lori was and still is the weakest of the family. Before Lori started school she was a diabetic. She is the shortest of all of us, but despite her physical weaknesses and stature, she has attained great things. Over her fifty-six years she has become a registered nurse (she runs a cancer clinic in Caribou), and despite nearly losing her eyesight and having already lost her kidneys, she is still a shining example of a good sister. I wish we had been told more of Jesus' sisters because I can't imagine that he wasn't as proud of them as I am of Lori and Sylvia.

Sisters have gotten much negative press over the years, and I don't know about others, but as for me I am thankful that the good Lord decided to send a sister before me because she was a faithful forerunner in my formable years. And I am thankful that the good Lord decided to send a sister after me because she has been a wonderful example to me on how to press on when life gets difficult and when you are not blessed with good health. Both Jesus and I had sisters!

A BARK IN NAZARETH

Isaiah 56:10 ... bark ...

Did Jesus have a boyhood pet? Was there a neighborhood dog who was his best friend? In one of Jesus' most famous stories (the rich man and Lazarus Luke 16:31) neighborhood dogs are seen as comforting creatures (Luke 16:21). Jesus also believed in the philosophy first taught by Job: "But ask now the beasts and they shall teach thee . . . " (Job 12:7) I learned much in my boyhood from the friendly bark of a part collie, part German shepherd I called Rover.

I yearn for that appealing sound again. Many years ago my wife and I took care of a dog belonging to some friends of ours, but this dog didn't bark. It didn't yap, yelp, or yip either. At the same time we were dog sitting Nicky, we were cat sitting the cat of my wife's sister and the two animals became chummy. Not so the dog of my boyhood. Rover was a dog's dog. He loved to chase chickens and cats, and when he could get away with it, cows and cars. He barked at anything that moved except in the house where he was only allowed on cold nights and special occasions. His sound was refreshing, not irritating. He was the one stabilizing creature in a farmyard of constant activity He taught me how to slow down and take it easy. Did Jesus have such an instructor?

Rover's bark was a call to an unhurried lifestyle. His "bow wow" was a warning that life taken too seriously can bring on serious problems, and as my county cousin Clayton once wrote, "It is high time we take a lesson from man's best friend and listen to what he is telling us by his bark:

"Never pass up the opportunity to go for a joy ride.

Allow the experience of fresh air and the wind in your face to be pure ecstasy.

A BARK IN NAZARETH

When loved ones come home, always run to greet them.
When it's in your best interest, practice obedience.
Let others know when they have invaded your territory.
Take naps and stretch before rising.
Run, romp, and play daily.
Eat with gusto and enthusiasm.
Be loyal.
Never pretend to be something you're not.
If what you want lies buried, dig until you find it.
When someone is having a bad day, be silent, sit close by, and nuzzle them gently.
Thrive on attention and let people touch you.
Avoid biting when a simple growl will do.
On hot days, drink lots of water and lie under a shady tree.
When you're happy, dance around and wag your entire body.
Delight in the simple joy of a long walk.
No matter how often you're scolded, don't buy into the guilt thing and pout. Run right back and make friends."

AN OAK IN NAZARETH

EZEKIEL 6:13 ... UNDER every thick oak ...

Did Jesus have a favorite tree in his boyhood? Boys love trees for climbing and sitting under and playing around. The forests of my childhood farm were dominated by maple, pine, fir, and spruce, but scattered throughout these woods was the occasional oak. The mighty oak is a beautiful tree, and its position among the other trees of the farm was never questioned. These are some of the things I have observed about the oak tree.

First, every year during the fall season one can notice that the oak retains its crisp dried leaves long after the maple, elm, or the other trees of the forest have lost their leaves to the gusty winds and driving rains of autumn. I too am facing the final days of fall. In just a few more days winter will come and with it the season of death. I admire the oak for hanging in there the longest. Oh, it will yield as all do to the inevitable, but it showed me that one needs not go willingly or happily into such a storm. I have always resisted those situations I don't like. Life sometimes plays strange games with you, but like the oak, I shall hang on to my leaves of summer as long as I can. I will not easily be drawn into a time I care not to experience. Did Jesus hang on to Nazareth for that very reason?

Second, I noticed that even the strong winds and the deep snows of winter cannot completely strip the oak's bough. Even during the worst part of the year, the oak clings to its dignity with a tenacity that puts the human race to shame. Every trial and adversity is faced with grace and determination that spring will come and this humiliating season will soon be over. The lifeless leftovers of a glorious summer season are maintained as the mantle of white carpets the ground around the proud oak. Who of us has not been humiliated by the evils of a cold temptation or the frost of a brother's fall? I face such a season as I recall the homestead oak. The seasons on the northern fringes of Maine made the oak tough, and that same climate has made me tough as well. As the oak survived the worst, so did Jesus.

Third, I noticed as springtime progresses, the scene for the oak begins to change. Fresh little buds start appearing at the tips of the twigs. Soon the dried remnants of the preceding season drop away, and a surge of new life brings the glory of the oak back again. I have that same confidence with the winter season I am now going through. Despite my outward appearance, within dwells the ability to be revived, restored, and resurrected. A new leaf will push off those old ones, and when the process is through, the pitiful state will be forgotten in the gorgeous renewal of a fully leafed oak, and for me a new life as well. Jesus came to demonstrate the greatest new life of them all—bodily resurrection. Had He seen it first in an oak in Nazareth?

A HARVEST IN NAZARETH

Proverbs 6:8 . . . and gathereth her food in the harvest.

Over and over I found myself standing near a fruit tree when I was a lad on my family's farm in Maine. The homestead was covered with apple orchards and isolated apple trees. I often went looking for fruit, but either found no fruit or fruit that was not ripe. However, patience and perseverance would be rewarded as the time of harvest approached. Did Jesus have similar experiences? Is this why He often spoke of the lessons of the harvest when He began to preach?

I can still see myself sitting on a large limb of an apple tree with the branches loaded with the fruit of fall. It was then I learned that the hard work of pruning in the spring was now paying off and delay wasn't something evil, but something good. I learned often that impatience only brought a bitter taste to your mouth as you bit into an apple too soon. These were the lessons and more I learned from the fruit trees of my childhood. Jesus already knew about the teaching of the harvest and the importance of timely picking.

I still stand amazed how much practical wisdom could be found in the fruit tress of the farm. We were a potato and dairy operation, not a fruit farm. The fruit trees were only a hobby of those who had come before us on the 720-acre farm in Aroostook County, Maine. Granted, a small percentage of the apples were used for apple pies, apple sauce, and the occasional apple fight with a cousin or two, but the majority of apples were left for the white-tail deer and other creatures of the forest. Yet during the days I mowed under the branches or played hide and seek behind the trunks, I learned many a valuable lesson that has stood me in good standing to this day. Here are some of them: (1) Pruning doesn't harm the tree, but makes it more productive, and so does God's chastening (Hebrews 12:5–7); (2) the

A HARVEST IN NAZARETH

first fruits are not always the best fruits. One must give time for maturing as with life's fruits (Luke 8:15); (3) Keep looking up and keep climbing because the best fruit is at the top of the tree (Philippians 3:13,14); (4) When you're asked by another to harvest some fruit, remember there is a sweet reward waiting in the end because of your labor (John 4:35–38); (5) Remember, two harvesting can gather more fruit then one, and if you're caught up a tree and out on a limb, they can always help get you down (Ecclesiastes 4:9–12); (6) Don't forget, as you're harvesting you are relieving the burden of another (Galatians 6:2).

When I was a kid, all I knew of fruit was the fruit. I picked from the tree. Now I see that there was another kind of "fruit" that could also be picked and gathered from the trees of my boyhood. Did Jesus see similar lessons in a Nazareth harvest of grapes, dates, or figs?

A CEDAR IN NAZARETH

PSALMS 80:10 THE BOUGHS thereof were like the goodly cedars.

Recently, I heard a title to a movie called Snow Falling on Cedar. The idea of the picturesque name began to generate a few thoughts of my own. I have not seen the movie and have no knowledge of its plot, but this is what I learned from snow falling on cedar on my boyhood homestead. By Jesus' speaking style, we know he used what the people could understand to explain heavenly truth. The cedar was a familiar sight in Galilee, and, yes, it did snow in Nazareth.

Having had the privilege of living in a region where there was plenty of snow and plenty of cedar trees has allowed my imagination to run wild. The cedar tree has some admirable characteristics especially when covered by snow.

First, the lustrous beauty of the very image of a cedar tree covered with snow. There is an attractiveness that draws one to such a sight. I loved to snowshoe in my youth and often after a heavy but fluffy snow I would trek out to the cedar grove behind my father's massive cow barn. It was a sight to behold and still is. (Job 38:2)

Second, the delightful fragrance when standing under a cedar tree blanketed in white. There is a delicate aroma that is caught under the bowed branches of a cedar tree. Despite the cold and frosty air, the perfume of the cedar trees permeates the grove. It is a smell that covers you, and you can breathe it in all the way home. (Song of Solomon 5:15)

Third, the remarkable durability of the cedar to take the weight of the heaviest Maine snow. I have seen with my own eyes cedar branches many feet above the ground touching the ground after a weighty snow. I have wondered why these limbs didn't break, yet when the wind picks up or the sun strengthens and the snow cover is either blown away or melts away, those same bowed branches spring back to full height and reach, a miracle of Christ's creation. (Psalms 104:16)

Fourth, the fruitful flourishing of the cedar to reproduce that creates that cluster of cedars known as groves. A single cedar covered in snow is a sight to behold, but an entire grove of cedar trees so clothed is almost heavenly. Like a chapel in the woods, the closeness of the cedars allows one to crawl underneath and in some places find a snow-free piece of soil. I have on occasion found such places to rest even in the middle of a severe winter. Out and away from the wind, the cedar grove even isolates one from the bitter cold temperatures outside. If it is possible, it seems almost warm under "snow falling on cedar." (Amos 2:9)

Fifth, the enduring quality of the cedar is legendary. It is impervious to decay. It is repulsive to insects. It is purifying to the forest. It is strong in its uses. It is inspiring in its applications, especially when one gets an image in his mind of "Snow Falling on Cedar" as you have just witnessed. (Psalms 92:12)

Certainly, Jesus saw this for he created the cedar!

A SEED IN NAZARETH

MARK 4:31 It is like a grain of mustard seed, which, when it is sown in the earth, is less than all the seeds that be in the earth.

One of the greatest marvels of nature, in my opinion, is the growth of a huge tree from a tiny seed. I have found a sermon in that seed from my days on the family's farm. Is that where Jesus got his idea for his "mustard seed" sermon?

When a tree seed, any tree seed, is stimulated by water and warmth, it begins to geminate. From that germination a growth process begins to change that tiny seed. Very small rootlets start to emerge from the shell of that seed and begin to bury themselves in the ground upon which the seed fell. That burial ground might be directly under the mother tree or miles away. Carried by wind or creature, the infant seed finds rest and root. As the seed continues to plunge downward, a slender shoot pushes upward towards the light of the sun. Instinctively, the seed knows it needs both the nurture of the ground and of the sun. From these two sources the seedling receives the air and moisture needed to turn into a sapling. As its roots extend deeper into the soil of its birth, its leaves will spread themselves closer to the sun until a stately tree takes its place with the other monarchs of the forest. The process was Christ-made.

It is the growth and maturing of the seed that my sermon comes. First, there must be a trust in the perfect will of the Creator of where the seed will land. The seed has no will or choice in the soil of its birth, and neither do we. Where we are born and to whom we are born are not for us to ponder. Ours is to grow and mature where we start. Second, there must be an acceptance of the environment the seed is to grow in. The climate or the surroundings must be accepted. The seed doesn't ponder its fate, but simply starts growing where it is, and so must we. Today, we have so many

A SEED IN NAZARETH

people being convinced that they have been given a bad deal in relationship to their parents, their social status, and their racial distinction. Take a lesson from the seed and be all that you can be in what you are. Third, there must be a willingness to become the kind of tree the seed came from. If a cedar seed, then a cedar tree. If a pine seed, then a pine tree. Implanted in the heart of every seed is the nature of the tree to be produced. It seems as if only human beings are apt to change their very nature. Created in the image of the Creator, the human seed was quick to conform to the image of a creation rather than the Creator. How could a holy and pure creation planted in a perfect environment turn out so ugly? Answer: sin. In an attempt to blame the Creator or the environment, we the seeds of God have failed to look within. It is time we get back to the nature of the seed that was planted in everyone of us. If I could find a sermon in a seed, couldn't Christ? And He did. (Matthew 13:1–9)

THE STEADFASTNESS OF NAZARETH

Colossians 2:5 ... the steadfastness of your faith in Christ.

In my numerous walks by trees on my family's homestead in Perham, Maine, I have come across the battered and beaten tree. I have come to see in that bent and bruised tree a beauty that is called by Paul "the steadfastness of your faith in Christ," and I call it "the steadfastness of Nazareth."

There is a loveliness that only comes through adversity and attack. The tree sheltered in a grove or protected in a forest is a good tree, but a tree exposed to the raging wind or the driving snow develops a character all its own. Stormy weather might cause some damage, but the tree that survives the strain will contain the better wood. I have always been drawn to and stirred by the solitary tree that finds its footing and roots itself in the harsh and harassed piece of land and the isolated tree that grows alone clinging only to the ground of its birth. There is no other to protect it, and it must face and fight alone the water and wind of every stormy night and every hot and dry day. Sturdily it stands in the path of hail and sleet; steadfastly it stands against drought and flood; stately it stands exposed to perilous season and unprotected attacks, and so did Jesus in life.

Unlike man or mammal, the tree can't move when times get tough. Rooted in one spot, it soon learns it must bow and bend to survive the onslaught of summer's sun, fall's fall, winter's wind, and spring's storms. The stress and strain of environmental pressure must be combined with the formidable setting that the tree finds itself in. Disease and damage take its toll as the rings multiply, but the solitary tree remains as generation after generation of man and mammal pass away. Wind-twisted and storm-tossed, the tree has taken on a shape distorted and distinctive. To scare the outward

THE STEADFASTNESS OF NAZARETH

view, what the ice of a late winter storm didn't do, the gale force winds of an early fall storm would do. The tree cannot keep living from branches and bark destroyed twigs and trunk damaged, and limbs and leaves dropped. Its wood is impregnated with pitch and resins that are lubricants of healing for every wound that has been inflicted upon it. This fluid allows it to bend, but not break. Its fibers allow it to yield, but not be yanked from its place. Its flexibility allows it to bow under the weight of a winter's snow, but also allows it to spring back with the advent of spring. So did Jesus.

I have learned so much from my solitary tree that I dare not give in to my days of hardship. To the average onlooker I too may seem contorted and bruised by life's storms. My exterior may seem damaged and bent from lives blows, but I, like the tree, have learned that what I can't change I can conquer. Did not Jesus teach, "In the world ye shall have tribulation: but be of good cheer; I have overcome the world." (John 16:33) Jesus overcame Nazareth.

THE SPRING OF NAZARETH

Psalms 87:7 ... ALL my springs are in Thee.

I have already mentioned that one of the assets that caused the early residents to settle in Nazareth was the discovery of a sweet, abundant spring. When my forefathers settled in what would become known as Perham, Maine, there were no building or roads or any sign of civilization in the virgin track of woods. That piece of northern Maine forest was divided up into 160-acre lots and sold to any adventurous soul strong enough to clear the land and start a farm. One of my ancestor's first discoveries on this new land was a hidden spring, a special spot that remains to this day over 147 years later—a Nazareth style spring.

It was rocked and became the primary source of fresh water to the new farmhouse located just down the slope from it. Eventually, it was gravity fed into the first permanent framed house built in Perham. By the time I came along in the early 1950s, the spring had been replaced by a well. It remained hidden in a small grove of trees that had been left as a hedge against the bitter winds of winter. I was nearly a teenager before I rediscovered that ancient spring and uncovered its special secret.

I was playing with my cousins when I came across the unique grouping of stones. Ferns and small bushes had grown up around the rocks almost hiding it from view. As we explored its makeup and its construction, we discovered that it was not a very deep well, but it was still a flowing spring. A small pit had been dug to create a tiny pool. Flat stones had been placed around it to protect it from foreign objects falling into it and a top to keep the leaves out. Even the old pipe that led to the house over a quarter of a mile away could be seen below the waterline. Its water was still cold and sweet, so what was its secret? How was it possible that so much water could be concentrated in this one isolated spot? Where did this clear, pure water

THE SPRING OF NAZARETH

come from especially when you considered that the spring was not located near any other source of water? It was on a flatland piece of ground so there was no hope of run-off rain to feed it.

The source of this spring didn't lie in the great skies that arched above it, but in the depth of earth that lay beneath it. It was not the weather systems that brought mist, snow, rain, and moisture from above, but a reservoir of water located deep in the land beneath the farm. Gleaned from all over the farm, water from above filtered through stone and soil and eventually flowed to this special spot. Hidden rivers are born of God and placed by Him at critical places for the needs of His creation. I have often wondered if my ancestors would have stayed and built on that spot if they hadn't found that underground river or if that spring had not been there. What was true of Nazareth was true of Perham, and now I know "all my springs are in Thee."

THE RIDGE OF NAZARETH

PSALMS 65:10 THOU WATEREST the ridges thereof abundantly . . .

One of the faulty concepts that have crept into our society is that a man cannot stand alone and survive. Without support an individual will be unproductive and useless to the world. Prosperity and peacefulness are impossible without the group. This precept is simply false, especially for those courageous souls who have the will be stand in the open, set apart from the team, despite the blast of scorn and scoffing from a cynical planet. So where did I learn this truth? I learned it from an isolated tree that still stands today on a rugged ridge just east of my father's house. Jesus stood on a similar ridge in Nazareth.

Well above the valley floor stands a ridge that runs along the eastern border of my family's farm in Perham, Maine. It still stands thick with trees because of my father's desire that the last untouched grove of forest left on our 720-acre farm remain unharvested. There among the spruce, maple, and poplar stands a lonely pine. There it clings alone to the rocky ridge it took root in over a hundred years or more ago. There it incorporated its will to live despite the demise of its kind on that same ten-acre ridge. Its hardness, toughness, and ruggedness have withstood every gale and storm, even though it has no mutual support structure. Its exquisite beauty is in its uncompromising stand. It is battered and bruised in places. It is twisted and trimmed in other places. The weight of a northern Maine snow has removed a few lower limbs not strong enough to bear the winter burden, but its trunk as a whole stands straight and strong.

What is it that we should learn from this one pine standing defiant on that country ridge? Growth has nothing to do with external turmoil, but an internal willingness to survive. Maturity has nothing to do with external testing's, but an internal need to keep on living. Survival has more to do with self then society. How much are you willing to take? How much are you willing to endure? How much are you willing to put up with? The fierce blasts may come and probably will come, but no wind to date has affected that lone pine. I take great encouragement from that. I too have been blasted by criticism and ridicule, yet I still stand. I am still in my called profession though there are those who have proclaimed my unworthiness. A little over a year ago it looked like the pine and its neighbors on the ridge were going to be cut. It was then my father stepped in and prevented the harvesting of the trees along the ridge. The day may come when there is no one to resist the cutting.

For me that lone pine is an illustration of the life of Christ in Galilee. From beginning to the end, Jesus was always standing alone on some ridge in either Nazareth or Jerusalem.

A ROOSTER IN NAZARETH

MARK 13:35 ... AT the cockcrowing ...

Having been a preacher for nearly two-thirds of my life, I have a hard time not using as illustrations in my sermons what happened during the first third of my life, as did Jesus. I have over the years thought of so many lessons I learned on my family's farm in northern Maine that have spiritual overtones. A case in point is a recent study of Peter's denial of Jesus during Christ's trial. Most of you know the story from Sunday school, and how Peter was reminded of Jesus' prophecy concerning his betrayal by the cockcrowing. Many concepts and precepts can be gleaned from a cock-a-doodle-do and a rooster in Nazareth.

Crow Concept 1: The rooster rises early to use his God-given talent for crowing. How important it is for us to also exercise our Spirit-given gifts every day. The earlier the better! (Romans 12:1)

Crow Concept 2: The rooster doesn't stop crowing because he can't sing like a canary. It is so very important for us to tell and sing the message of God's love whether we have a good voice or not. A warning is more often heard by a sharp shout then a sweet song. (I Corinthians 12:22)

Crow Concept 3: The rooster enthusiastically and energetically cries out whether he is praised or not. God is looking for those of us that will earnestly tell and fervently talk of the coming dawn, a dawn that could be the "day of salvation" for our listener. (Ecclesiastes 9:10)

Crow Concept 4: The rooster awakens sleepers, a very unpopular thing to do, but also very necessary. No one likes to be awakened by the sudden cry of a cock. We would prefer to stay asleep, and so it is with a world asleep in their sins. It takes our warning that "the day of the Lord" is at hand and judgment isn't far behind. (I Thessalonians 5:6–8)

Crow Concept 5: The rooster is the proclaimer of good news, the arrival of a new day with great opportunities for good. Day brings with it a privilege to work for the Lord. We need to work because the "night is coming when no man will work" or crow. (Romans 13:11, 12)

Crow Concept 6: The rooster is dependable and persistent in his task. Spreading the good news is not a once a week job or once a lifetime occupation, but a daily duty that must be faithfully seen to and through. (Ephesians 6:18)

Crow Concept 7: The rooster never murmurs about having to do the same common call every morning. Telling the "old, old story" has become trying to some. There are even others that would change the crow of the Christian. Only when the good Lord changes the call of the cock will the call of the Christian be changed. (II Timothy 4:2)

Since I began to ponder on "a rooster in Nazareth," I wondered if Jesus remembered that Nazareth cock when he told Peter about his up and coming denial.

A WIND IN NAZARETH

PSALMS 103:16 FOR THE wind passeth over it, and it is gone . . .

    I read once of a certain German baron who pulled a series of wires between two towers of his mountain castle. His hope was to create a large Aeolian harp, a musical instrument that makes a marvelous sound when air is blown through its strings. After the wires were strung, the baron waited for the lovely music, but at first there was no sound because the air was still. Soon, however, as the gentle evening breeze began to blow through the valley, he caught the first faint notes coming from the huge harp. Still unimpressed, he waited and soon discovered that the most harmonic strains didn't happen until the strong winter winds swept across the wires. It was only then the valley below filled with wonderful sounds. I never lived in a castle and my family's farm wasn't located on a mountainside, but like Jesus in Nazareth I heard the music of the wind, too.

    I remember clearly the haunting music of a winter northeaster blowing through the cracks in my upstairs bedroom window. It was a calming tune and a scary strain all at the same time, especially if my sister would choose that moment to jump me. Did Jesus and his sister do such things?

    I remember hearing the pleasant melody of a springtime zephyr blowing through the huge barn doors. The wind felt warm after a hard winter, and the deep music created by the wide passageway through the barn was peaceful. The sound of the Holstein herd in the stalls mixed well creating a potpourri unmatched. Where did Jesus listen to the wind?

    I remember listening to the gentle breezes on a hot summer night blowing quietly through the trees surrounding my homestead home. I had come to the front porch for some cooling air and the evening concert. Added to the harmony of the bull frogs in the local pond and the night crickets, this was a piece of music that has always been on my Top Ten List. Did Jesus have his favorite "wind tune?"

I remember best the autumn gale that would blow every fall during potato harvest season. Some days it was warm from the southwest and other days it was cold from the northwest. The composition it played depended on which field we were gleaning at the time. If we were down on the Paul place, the music would be open and light. Sheltered by the steep side hill, the wind couldn't build much strength. If we were in the open country of the Home Place, the wind would howl around the potato barrels and farm equipment. If we were picking on the Russell Place, the surrounding forest would create a new measure to the continuing music of the wind. Did Jesus make note of such times with the wind?

I didn't realize it then, but I do now. I had many an opportunity to listen to the music created by the wind that blew across the strings of my life. All it takes is a listening ear and the windy world around us in Nazareth.

THE CRICKETS OF NAZARETH

Hosea 2:18 . . . with the creeping things of the ground . . .

One of the sounds I remember most of my childhood is the noise of the crickets during a mid-summer's night's rest on the porch. It wasn't until I came across these verses in the Psalms that I discovered what the crickets were doing during their dusk vigil. "Let them praise the name of the Lord: for He commanded, and they were created . . . Praise the Lord from the earth . . . creeping things . . . " (Psalms 148:5, 7, 10) Jesus heard the crickets of Nazareth praising him in his boyhood town.

The cricket, of which there are 1400 species, was created to praise the Lord. In its own unique way the evening cricket is praising the name of its creator. Someone has said, "Nature is like an outstretched finger pointing toward God," and the cricket points one to God through its amazing voice of praise. Yet the cricket is not a vocalist, but a violinist. The cricket makes music by running the inner edges of its front legs together. If its front legs are used for "jamming," its back legs are used for jumping. This tiny creature of less than an inch can leap one hundred times its own length, but its fame is in its front legs. The Bible tells us about its "praise concerts," but science has also discovered another bit of wisdom it proclaims in its evening serenade. The cricket also tells the temperature. If you count the chirps it makes in fifteen seconds and then add that number to 37, you will get the evening temperature of the place where you are listening to your favorite cricket canon. Isn't God's science amazing?

Another interesting fact I have learned about the cricket is that only the male's chirp. The females only listen through the ears she has in her front legs. The cricket delights in this instrumental song of praise and is hardly ever silent. This creeping creature is sometimes called the Chinese canary because of the ancient Chinese fascination with God's marvelous musician. The Chinese would keep crickets in cages and would feed them their favorite insect. They even had a technique for making their crickets play. By tickling the cricket's hind legs, it would begin chirping wildly with its front legs. Little did I know as I enjoyed the sound of the crickets with my family that I was listening to one of God's great creations of praise?

So the next time you have a chance to take a few minutes to listen to the local crickets, remember this little poem from an anonymous poet. **"Creeping things show forth His glory, each their task He did ordain; for His greatness and His wisdom; all His wondrous works proclaim!"** I believe that listening to praise by another is also praise itself. Whether from a creature or a Christian, God loves being praised, either in action of simply listening. Jesus was also praising his Father when he listened to the crickets.

THE ANTS OF NAZARETH

Proverbs 30:25 The ants . . .

In my boyhood barnyard creatures could be found of every size. We had plenty of chickens, pigs, cats, dogs, and of course cows, seeing the farm had a dairy. But as a child, I watched with great interest the ants on the side lawn. I can't believe Jesus didn't also watch the ants of Nazareth, one of His most amazing creations.

In the lawn by the front hedge were a number of small mounds of soil. Each time I would mow that section of the lawn I would run over these hills of earth. The largest was just a few inches high with barely a diameter of over a couple of feet. These tiny plateaus were built from the ground up by thousands and thousands of ants moving millions of grains of sand from underground tunnels. I must admit one of my pleasures as a kid was to cut off the tops of these mounds with the blade of my mower and then watch these tiny creatures race from their holes to attack whatever had disrupted their world. They confronted the farmer's son, but there was little they could do but rebuild, and that is exactly what they did because by the next time I mowed that part of the lawn the ant hill was as big or bigger than the time before. It took a number of years, but I learned that the ant was put there on my side lawn to teach me something, not to entertain me.

It was my dad who told me of Solomon's instruction to "go to the ant" (Proverbs 6:6) and learn something. Thereafter, I would stop for a moment or two and watch the ant instead of harassing the ant. I found out the ant was untiring and certainly not lazy. I never saw a lazy ant. Every one was always hurrying and never dragging behind. I found the ant to be industrious and diligent. Besides not being lazy, I saw no loafers because each ant seemingly had a purpose, and they were busily working towards that goal. It wasn't long before I learned the simple ambition on the mind of the ant was preparation for a Maine winter. As I cut the early grass of spring, the ant was making stores for winter. As I mowed the deep lawn of summer, the ant was laying up for the onset of snow. As I finished mowing the lawn for the last time in early fall, the ant "gathereth her food in the harvest."

When I was a teenager, I finally realized why my dad had taught me the lesson of the ant. As I looked around my world, I discovered that my homestead was run much like that side lawn ant hill. There was no fighting and absolutely no loafing on the farm. Each member of our extended family had a job, and we did it quickly and with purpose because we too were facing a tough Maine winter. And like the ant, by the time the first wintry blast hit, we had stored enough to feed us and our animals during the long Maine winter. Did Jesus see through the ants of Nazareth the shortness of his time and the importance of finishing his course quickly?

A PLOUGHING IN NAZARETH

Isaiah 28:24 Doth the plowman plow all day to sow? Doth he open and break the clods of his ground?

Jesus was the son of a carpenter, but he must have watched on occasion the numerous farmers in the area because he used a lot of farming illustrations in his parables and sermons. One of my most favorite jobs on the family farm was ploughing. I wonder if Jesus ever helped the plowman.

I enjoyed the harvest season on the family farm in northern Maine, but I looked forward with much pleasure to something that always followed harvest, ploughing. Once the fields of potatoes were picked and the fields of oats were gleaned, we hitched the plows to the tractors and ploughing season would begin. Actually, what we were doing was getting an early start on spring. Dad never ploughed a field without the intention of sowing it in the spring. In all my years on the homestead, I never felt closer to the land then when I was ploughing. There is something about ploughing that makes you one with the earth? We didn't plough every field on the farm, only those worth cultivating. Dad never wasted his time ploughing land that would never see the planter. It was the fertile fields that got his attention, and all too soon, for me, we were done because once the field was ploughed it was left to rest until the warm sun of spring stirred it from its wintry sleep. Did Jesus watch this cycle unfold as well?

I haven't ploughed a field in years, but as I mediate on this necessary practice on the farm, I realize that in life a ploughing also must take place. God the great husbandman of the human race is also a plowman. An unknown author once wrote this challenging verse:

O God, wert thou ploughing
Thy profitless earth

A PLOUGHING IN NAZARETH

With the brave plough of Love,
And the sharp plough of Pain?
But hark to the mirth
Of wheat-field in harvest!
Dear Plougher, well worth
That ploughing, this yellow-gold grain?

As with my father, the heavenly Father does not plough without purpose. Where He ploughs, He will sow. It is at such times we feel He has forsaken us, but at that moment He is closest to us. The very reason He ploughs is evidence that He thinks us valuable, and as with natural ploughing, it only continues for a season. As with the land, we suffer for a moment as our soul is tossed and turned, but when the ploughing is over, there comes a season of rest and recovery. Then the sower will go forth to sow and the fruitless field will become a fruitful field at last. Ploughing is the price the land has to pay for a bountiful harvest, and travail of soul is the price we must sometimes pay for a marvelous spiritual harvest. This is what Jesus taught? I believe it was!

A SHOWER IN NAZARETH

ZECHARIAH 10:1 ASK YE of the Lord rain in the time of the latter rain; so the Lord shall make bright clouds, and give them showers of rain, to every one grass in the field.

When Jesus lived in Nazareth, he was limited by the same forces that played against each other throughout the region. One of the constant concerns was enough rain. The vineyards couldn't produce without timely rain. The crops of Nazareth couldn't grow without the early and the latter rains. Everything and everyone in that Galilee town was dependent on the periodic arrival of the rain clouds. I remember on my family's farm in northern Maine that a mid-summer shower was a gift sent directly from God Himself.

Sometimes, when I was a boy, I would hear my mother and father talking across the kitchen table about the need of rain. I even recall my dad praying for rain before he thanked the good Lord for our food. He would ask for rain and pray for rain, but all that would come was a shower. I would ask myself, "Had God lost control of the weather?" I had been taught in Sunday school that God was in control, and that what we ask for and need will be provided. Why then did God send a few drops of water when the farm needed a downpour of water? Was my father's faith weak? Was there sin the camp? Were we somehow out of the will of God? Perhaps Dad shouldn't have planted potatoes in the spring? I learned before I left the farm that not one of those reasons was valid. There was no sin, and we were in His will. He was still in control, and my father's faith was enough. What I learned through a homestead shower was that God sometimes hides His plans so that we are forced to live by faith.

During my twenty-one summers on the homestead I never saw a year that showers were not enough. There were those people that begged for more and spent their time saying, "What if . . . ," but I never saw the potato plants die or the Holstein herd thirsty. I also never heard my father complain after an afternoon shower that what had been given from above wasn't enough. I knew he would have liked a bit more, but he seemed content in the fact that his Heavenly Father thought it was enough for that day. Perhaps, there in is the lesson. If we look at the summer one day at a time, we would say not enough. But when we see the season and how it turned out, we rejoice in the fact that it was enough. Granted, if we would have had a hot, muggy summer on the coast of Maine, my front lawn would have died, but a cool summer with a few showers was enough to keep everything green, and God knew that.

I learned in the summers of my youth that a God-sent shower was worthy of praise, and that the good Lord has promised us "the early and latter rains" even if those rains came in the form of showers. "In every life a little rain must fall," and if that rain is a shower, then we have been truly blessed above all measure. Nazareth knew this as well.

CLOUDS OVER NAZARETH

Psalms 105:39 He spread a cloud for a covering . . .

I am writing this "Another Day in Nazareth" on a cloudy day on the coast of Maine. Most people don't like cloudy days, but I have come to appreciate a "cloud covering."

I, like many people, always thought a cloudy day was something mankind could do without, but I learned on the family farm that a cloudy day is necessary to maintain a balance in nature. Think about it. In what area of the world does the sun always shine? Deserts and wastelands. If the clouds never come then the rains wouldn't either. If the clouds didn't shade us on occasion then the sun would burn us up eventually. Mankind has discovered that there is "a silver lining behind every cloud," and here is the silver I mined from my memories on another day in my Nazareth.

I remember winter clouds for the snow they brought. I am not a winter sports person, but I have always loved a good snowstorm. Is there anything more calming then to see the dark clouds gathering in the early afternoon? A wintry night's snow is both limiting and exciting. It limits our travel, but it allows us a night inside. Sure, a snowy, cloudy day creates a bit more work, but it also gives us a chance to slow down. If there is anything I like, it is a slower pace, and a cloud with snow in it can do just that.

I remember spring clouds for the warm showers they brought. It wasn't until the early rains came that the potato plants really began to grow. The farm plants certainly needed the warm sun to shine, but sun without showers is a killing combination, not a growing association. The rain might spoil a little league game, but it could always be made up. A spring without water never could.

I remember summer clouds for their comfort. A popular misconception about northern Maine is that it never gets hot in the summertime. I still can remember those hay days in late July and August. It seemed the best time to hay was the worst time to work. The sun that made the hay would weary the laborer, but the good Lord was always kind to send along those covering clouds every once in a while. For just a few minutes the white, puffy clouds would block out the sun and give a weary soul a break from the exhausting heat.

I remember autumn clouds because of their radiant colors. With the onset of fall foliage, the clouds over harvest fields were brilliant. In the early morning as one rose before sunrise to start picking potatoes, the clouds would often be gray and lowering, but without rain. As the day progressed the clouds would take on a whitish color against the autumn blue sky. Then as the sun would set slowly in the west those same clouds would take on a heavenly pink color.

As the boy Jesus watched the clouds gather over Nazareth, did he remember the days when "a cloud by day" was His habitat (Exodus 13:21–22) as He travelled with the Israelites to Canaan?

LAUGHING IN NAZARETH

PSALMS 2:4 . . . THAT sitteth in the Heavens shall laugh . . .

If Jesus laughed in heaven then I am sure he laughed in Nazareth. Jesus knew that **"a merry heart doeth good like a medicine."** (Proverbs 17:22) I remember the first time I came across this proverb by Solomon, and I remember the first person I thought of. Who did Jesus think of, his Father?

Laughter has become to most of the world a commercial product. The entertainment industry has marketed well this God-given ability to laugh. Hilarious humor draws great crowds. Laughter meters register the success or failure of many a performer. The problem with most of the world's laughter is that it is very shallow, hardly getting above the surface of the gutter. Sometimes it is a fake and is only heard to cover up a hurt or a wrong. The world has been taught that one can only laugh at something dirty or something degrading. I am so glad that when I was young, I learned what true laughter was, and that it wasn't something to be ashamed of or hid. Jesus believed this before I did.

How my dad could laugh. I can still hear his early laughter in my ear, even these many years later. My dad's laugh was a bubbly giggle that comes from irrepressible joy and uncontrolled glee. Dad could erupt in a roar over anything. However, the first person I remember that could really make Dad laugh was Red Skeleton. He was one of the first real famous TV comedians. My dad use to watch his show and usually before it was over he was crying because he was laughing so hard. The reason Dad laughed so hard because there was only clean humor on television in those days. Those were the days you could sit down with your kids and watch a comedy show together. Those were the days before indecency and immorality took over the comedy business. Those were the days before Sodom replaced Mayberry. Those were the days when hem lines and bust lines were decent, and the jokes were under control as in Nazareth.

Dad's was a joyful laugh. It came from a heart that knew that laughter was a medicine. Don't get me wrong. Dad was a very serious man, but he knew how to laugh at life and himself. Another image I have of my dad is that of him sitting in my Grandfather Barton's apartment in Presque Isle one Friday night after grocery shopping. My grandfather snapped a picture of Dad while he was reading a magazine that must have contained a humorous cartoon or story. The smile on his face and the broad grin revealed the true state of Dad's nature that night. I have often wondered over the years if this is one of the reasons my dad led such a healthy life. Dad always worked hard and laughed hard. Could that be the reason he had such a merry heart?

I don't know what the boy Jesus laughed at, but I do know in the normal activities of a small country town there was always enough events and conversations to laugh at.

AN AUTUMN IN NAZARETH

ECCLESIASTES 3:2 . . . A time to die . . .

Maybe it's because I am feeling my age, but this past autumn was different in so many ways. I mourned during autumn the falling of the leaves, the passing of warm temperatures, and the gradual disappearance of the birds. How did Jesus feel that last autumn in Nazareth? Recently, I came across this poem by an anonymous poet who captured that last autumn in Nazareth.

> How sadly beats the heavy autumn rain;
> How mournful drives the wind among the trees;
> Along the shore the weary sailor sees
> The waves roll in that send him out again;
> The birds are restless in the scattered leaves,
> The clouds move wildly on in massy fold,
> And all the outer world, or earth, or air
> But yesterday so warm, so fair
> Is changed, and in a night, to drear and cold.
> Now goes the gold autumn far away;
> Now nearer comes the winter to my door;
> And thus doth nature, working evermore,
> Create new life from changes and decay.
> O Christ! Who in the hall of Pilate bore
> For me the scourge and mocking, for Thy sake
> Fill up the daily loss in life of mine
> With Thy life! So shall love divine
> Out of the changing the unchanging make.

AN AUTUMN IN NAZARETH

The Blackstone homestead was a great place to watch the leaves turn, but a sad place to watch the leaves fall. With the rising of the wind and the pounding of the rain, the leaves quickly piled up around the house on the Blackstone Road and with them the end of Indian summer. Annually, God demonstrates the great precept of death and decay, but just before the final leaf falls, God illustrates something even more glorious. God never intended His nature to die drably. At this time of the year, God dresses His creation in the gorgeous gowns of autumn. The brightest colors of the year are seen in the final days of fall. The fullest hues can be witnessed in the final hours of autumn. I don't know if it was just me, but this fall on the coast of Maine was the most brilliant I can remember. I watched the gaily colored leaves dance up the street on a southerly breeze in front of my home, and for the first time in sixty-seven falls I marveled in the rich robes as they fell from the neighborhood trees. I saw for the first time that when nature dies, it dies gloriously!

The same can be said of the Christ. Was there ever a more glorious death then the one from Calvary's brow? In the horror there was divine beauty that causes one to look, stare, and rejoice at the same time one mourns the death.

A HEN IN NAZARETH

LUKE 13:34 . . . AS a hen doth gather her brood under her wing . . .

    The evening shadows lay stretched across the dirty barn floor. At the far end of the second floor of this huge cow barn is a wooden enclosure accessed by a single door. On the other side of that door the Blackstone chickens await their supper. As I approach their domain, I can hear the chuckles and the pecks here and there near the door as the flock awaits my appearance because I am their provider. I take a deep breath because I don't like chickens and open the door. From every quarter the chickens move with haste to my side to get the grain I have in my hand because such is the manner of a flock of chickens at feeding time. Even in their natural desire to escape their prison, there is no attempt to pass through the wide-open door. Not one chick turns away and not one chicken eyes the door because all eyes are on the farmer's son and the meal and water he carries. Within seconds of my entering the pen they are crowded around my feet, all focused on their one primary and paramount occupation of being fed. The door is well open, and they have no interest in anyone or anything but me. Why? Because at that moment all they desire is within their pen, not without.

    As I ponder again this event that happened numerous times in my boyhood, I must admit I see it clearly now in a different light. Probably because I have been a preacher for too many years, I now see a wonderful illustration to a divine precept. In John's picture of the New Jerusalem, he says this, "And the gates of it shall not be shut at all by day: for there shall be no night there." (Revelation 21:25) Because we don't live in defensive cities today, we miss the meaning here, but in the day of John this statement would have stood out to his readers. In his day the gates of the city were closed at night because an open gate would be a menace to the safety of the city. But with God within and having tasted of the food and freedom there, who would desire to run from God's pen? Like with the chickens in the Blackstone pen, we shall have all that we wish for and want within "and there shall in no wise enter into it anything that defileth." (Revelation 21:27)

The same Jesus of Nazareth that wished to gather his own like "a hen gathereth her chickens" (Matthew 23:37) will one day get His wish, but, unlike the first time when many fled and escaped at His first appearing, it shall not happen in His second coming. And for those of His own that will be taken to their new home in Heaven, they shall live in mansions with an open door in a city of open gates. What a beautiful picture of the liberty we will have there in Christ. No doubt this is a truth he experienced in feeding the chickens in Nazareth. Could this be another teaching of Jesus that came from a boyhood encounter in Galilee?

WAITING IN NAZARETH

Psalms 62:1 Truly my soul waiteth upon God . . .

Homeward bound! Only those that have gone away and lived away can understand the thrill of being homeward bound.

As I pass my sixty-seventh year, I have now spent more years away from home then at home. I was born and raised in a small community called Perham in northern Maine. At 18 I finally left home to travel between Greenville, South Carolina, and Perham as I attended college. For a short time I went back to Perham for the winter of 1978/1979, but for the rest of my life I have lived somewhere else. Did Jesus have such feelings for Nazareth?

Often as I travel through the small towns leading to my hometown, I picture again the old homestead. As I leave Presque Isle for Crouseville, I get a vision of the home place. As I travel through Washburn heading for Duntown, I picture those I am going home to see and remember other memorable homecomings. I see my dad now standing beside the driveway as my sister and I pull in from our long drive from South Carolina. Dad has seen us turn the corner as he is heading for the barn to do his afternoon chores. With dirt on his hands, but a smile on his face, he greets us with, "How was the trip?" It seems that from my earliest recollection there was always somebody home to greet me when I came home. Whether it was from the local elementary school just three miles up the road or college 1500 miles down the road, I don't ever remember being "home alone."

I come from a long line of homebodies. Few Blackstones before me drifted far from home. Those of us who have don't like it. Our roots are deep in the dark soil of Perham, and there is just something inbred that causes us to gravitate back when we have been away too long. For some it is the place, but for me it is the people. My parents over 90 years called

WAITING IN NAZARETH

Perham home. No retirement to Florida for them. I have a brother that only lives a few miles away from the homestead and two sisters that live even closer. Then there is the myriad of uncles, aunts, and cousins that still live in the area. It takes a vacation just to see them all. And then there are my county friends.

As I get closer to my departure day and further way from my arrival date, I am beginning to imagine that is what heaven is going to be like. There beside the golden driveway stands my Grandfather Carroll with a "welcome home." There beside the river stands my dear father-in-law with a "Welcome home, son." There beside the throne is my Saviour, and He says, "Welcome, well done!" Heaven is home and, for us who gave our hearts to Christ years ago, we are homeward bound. I am closer today then I was when I started this journey from Perham, but I still pray that when that call finally comes, I will get to my heavenly home by way of my earthly home. I am waiting in Nazareth.

ALONE IN NAZARETH

MATTHEW 14:23 ... WHEN evening was done, He was there alone.

I am just a few months after turning sixty-seven. As I approach this age, I feel more and more like the prophets of old. Men like Jeremiah, Amos, and Micaiah, lone dissenters in ages when the majority said one thing, but their lone voices spoke the truth. As Jesus did in and after Nazareth.

There is an overwhelming tidal wave rolling across our land to conform. The spiritual mood of the church is to get along and to go along. I have for most of my life been pressured to adjust to the age and adapt to the times. However, I keep asking myself the question, "Adjust to what?" Adjust to the compromising going on in marital morals? Adjust to the coexisting going on with religious groups that don't believe in Jesus as the Son of God? Adjust to the conforming image of the modern worship system that is nothing other than a Hollywood make over? Adjust to the culture of Madison Avenue business practices in the church? I simple ask with Paul, " . . . what harmony is there between Christ and Belial?" (II Corinthians 6:15) If I learned anything from Jesus of Nazareth, it is that the preacher has to be a soloist. Duets and trios might sound harmonious in proclaiming a song, but there will be nothing but trouble and tumult when it comes to presenting a sermon on truth.

I am getting more stubborn as I get older, but I like to think that it is a spiritual stubbornness. I refuse to be swept from the Rock on which I stand. I will resist the flood that would drown the old-fashion ways I believe in. I resent those that would try to silence this old voice by saying I am out of touch with the reality that now exists in the body of Christ. The way I see the problem is that the modern church is out of touch with its Head. We are arms and legs moving at our own will and not the will of God. We are speaking without a direct link to our Brain. We have tuned out the still small voice and have tuned into the popular message of the moment, but where does it say that we are to be popular? If Jesus' life teaches us anything, it is that we will be unpopular and without honor in our own country (Luke 4:24), county, or community. I learned this from a Loner from Nazareth.

So what has the world done in the past to silence the lone dissenter? John the Baptist was silenced when he had his head removed by a wicked queen. Elijah was silenced when he was named public enemy number one. Peter was silenced when he was confronted in public. Demas was silenced when he was paid off by the "love of this present world." (II Timothy 4:10) The ways are as varied as the men and women who stopped proclaiming "Thus saith the Lord!" I choose to follow those that can't be silenced. Abel kept on speaking through his blood. Jeremiah kept on writing despite the king burning his letters. Micaiah kept on prophesying through the fulfillment of his prediction and Jesus of Nazareth through His death.

A SWALLOW IN NAZARETH

PSALMS 84:3 . . . AND the swallow a nest for herself, where she may lay her young, even Thine altar, O Lord of host, my King, and my God.

Was Jesus a bird watcher in his boyhood in Nazareth? I believe he was. I observed the birds in my childhood in Perham. As I grew older, I learned from the Bible that God wants us to watch the birds. "But ask now . . . the fowls of the air, and they will tell thee . . . " (Job 12:77) or so said Job, the Old Testament saint. It was Jesus who confirmed this instruction when He said, "Behold the fowls of the air . . . " (Matthew 6:26) which includes a swallow in Nazareth.

I have read about the famous swallows of Capistrano. They are noteworthy because they always arrive on March 19 and leave on October 23. In 150 years these golden-breasted birds have spent their summers in the eaves of the old mission located in San Juan Capistrano. I have never been to San Juan Capistrano, but I too have witnessed the return of the swallows to my homestead farm in northern Maine. Each year (I never kept track of the dates) the swallows would return to spend their summers in the eaves of the old cow barn located next to my boyhood home. Did Jesus see such a sight?

For those who watch birds, it is an amazing phenomenon when one considers what it must take for this little bird to travel as it does. Some call it "mother nature" or "blind luck," but year after year has proved that it isn't luck. There has to be something supernatural going on to allow these small swallows such success. I was taught from a very early age that the birds were created on the fifth day of creation, and that it was the great Creator that put within these small creatures an instinct when to come north and when to travel south. The chickadee was created to survive a Maine winter, but not the swallow. Its very survival depends on its unusual timing. If they stay

A SWALLOW IN NAZARETH

too long, they will freeze, and if they come too early, they will starve. Frosty nights come early in northern Maine, and there is little natural food in early spring. Yet in my many years walking the barnyard, I never remember finding a swallow that had died from frostbite or starvation, usually it was the barn cat.

The sparrow seems to get most of the print in the bird magazines. Even the Bible only mentioned this marvelous bird a few times. Yet there is no denying that the Master bird watcher, God, has His eye on the swallow. His care for them is a lesson to His care of us. (Matthew 10:29–031) If He so guides the little swallow to a perfect landing at the perfect time, won't He also lead us? When will we as humans realize that if God takes time with the swallow's scheduling, will he not take time for ours? **"Trust in the Lord with all thine heart; and lean not to thy own understanding. In all thy ways acknowledge Him, and He will direct thy paths."** (Proverbs 3:5, 6) It starts in Nazareth.

THE GRANITE OF NAZARETH

MATTHEW 7:24 THEREFORE WHOSOEVER heareth these sayings of mine, and doeth them I will liken him unto a wise man, which built his house upon a rock.

Jesus taught the precept printed above, but have you ever asked yourself the question, where did the idea of building a house upon a rock come from? I suggest to you that it came from "another day in Nazareth." The rolling ridges and hallowed hills of Aroostook County have a natural quality of strength and solidarity about them, just like the hill that Nazareth was built upon. In reality, Aroostook County sets on a slab of gray granite. Those who live along the river valleys or have been blessed with land in the fertile plans barely see it, but for those of us whose family farms were hacked out of the virgin land of the hill country, granite close to the surface was a way of life as it was for the residents of Nazareth.

I never knew a time in my childhood when we didn't come across granite. I still see my dad coming in from plowing with a broken plow tooth. He had struck a piece of granite on the Paul Place. I remember while digging potatoes in the fall that Dad would dig very carefully over certain sections of certain fields. Over the years, Dad had learned where the State of Maine rose very close to the surface of the ground. He knew he had to lift the digger blade above the immovable granite or he would break a spade. There were those times when such an outcropping would present itself visibly in the middle of an oat field. I still recall when my grandfather would get out the dynamite and blast the top right off that old granite shelf. Was Nazareth's rock that visible as well?

Granite only bothered when it appeared in the fields we were planting. Granite exposed in the pasture was left alone. Cows have a great ability to feed around granite without any trouble or complaints. If we cut the pasture land, we had to be careful with the cutter blade lest we clip the granite ridges. But it was during such times I discovered that granite did have benefits because from it flowed the sweetest water on the planet. A deep granite spring (and the homestead had a number of them) produced a liquid that trickled to the surface and on a hot day in spring, summer, or autumn, we praised the virtue of granite. Did Jesus?

Over the years, I have wondered how my family has managed through six generations to remain on the land. Homes were built and potato houses and barns were raised that have stood the test of time. Now I see one of the reasons they have lasted—a firm foundation. I was taught as a lad that our faith was built upon the Rock, the Lord Jesus Christ (I Corinthians 10:4). When I was taught this concept in Sunday school, I didn't imagine a pebble or a stone or any ordinary rock, but I thought of the knoll on the Blackstone Road. My faith has endured nearly sixty years (I was born again in 1958) now because of building on the Rock. (I Corinthians 10:4)

HUMMINGBIRDS OVER NAZARETH

Zechariah 4:10 For who hath despised the day of the small things?

It was one of those warm and still late summer evenings in Nazareth. The sun was setting over the foothills to the west. Jesus' earthly world was engulfed in a yellow glow as he walked through the front door of his parent's home for a short interlude in the cooling air of the gathering night.

Jesus had come alone, but his dog (every boy needs a dog as I did in my youth) soon joined him as they took in the wonderful afterglow of another pleasant day in Nazareth. Jesus' dog would be no trouble because this best friend loved to relax by his feet. Jesus sat on the front steps as his dog lay out in front of him. They sat in complete silence, as good friends often do, hardly speaking a word, communicating as only a boy and his dog can do. The warm air was filled with the smells of the neighborhood, and the local bakery only added to the already wonderful aroma.

Suddenly, Jesus' nose took a back seat to his ear. Swiftly, a dark shadow shattered the solitude. A marvelous hummingbird streaked out of the sky in a power dive to the flowers near the door. The tiny bird seemingly feared neither boy nor beast. He shot past Jesus just inches from his head, and then paused in full flight as if to ask Jesus' permission to drink. Hovering there in midair, Jesus got a good look at the gallant creature that had invaded his space. As if to accept Jesus' non-verbal reply, the hummingbird darted to the flower and began to drink with wings still flapping at a hundred miles an hour. Within a few seconds the hummingbird was joined by its mate.

The two small birds hovered only a few more seconds before surging once again into full flight. In an instant, they were gone as they applied full power to their fragile wings and were soon lost from sight in the gathering darkness of the night. But Jesus wouldn't have to wait long before they returned. The nectar from the flower must have been too tempting for the pair because within minutes the whirring wings were back. With each twist and turn Jesus watched as they showed off with a series of aerial acrobatics. I also learned very early in life that man and all his machines have yet to match the humble hummingbird. What aircraft can maneuver like the hummingbird or hover like one either? The United States Marines are trying and are still failing after years of testing their humming, hovering plane. But on a cool summer's evening in the 1950s, I saw God's humming, hovering handiwork perform perfectly, just as Jesus did.

Stunned at their ability to hover and speechless at the speed by which they prefer to fly, these dynamic dynamos of flesh and feather have become one of my favorite creatures. I learned in my evenings in Nazareth (Perham) that Jesus' greatest creatures come in miniature.

FRUITLESS IN NAZARETH

MARK 11:13 AND SEEING a fig tree afar off having leaves, he came, if haply he might find any things thereon: and when he came to it, he found nothing but leaves . . .

Mark writes of this historical event late in Jesus' ministry, but I can't believe this was the first fruitless fig tree Jesus had seen. Could the roots of this lesson be found in a fruitless tree in "another day in Nazareth?"

I have found over the years that some of my favorite authors have also commented on this delusion of nature that has become a part of the world I live in. The first I would like to share with you on this matter of "leaving leaves" is from the great Scottish missionary Oswald Chambers. I quote, **"Leaves of a tree are a fruit, but not the fruit; they are for the nourishment of the tree itself. That is why in the autumn they push off and sink to the ground where they become disintegrated and are taken into the root again. The fruit proper is never for the tree itself. It is for the husbandman. Woe be to the man who mistakes leaves for fruit. The reason our Lord cursed the barren fig tree was because it stood as a symbol of leaves being proudly mistaken for fruit. When we mistake what we do for the fruit, we are deluded. What tells is not what we do, but what is produced by what we do!"** What is true about fruit trees ought to be true about Christians as well? Another Nazareth lesson.

The second to comment on the delusion is from a favorite American author, Phillip Keller, and I quote, **"To look at, it is a lovely tree. Ever since the first day I set eyes on this property, the handsome, young cherry tree just outside the breakfast nook aroused admiration. In spring and in summer its thick, dense foliage was a sight to behold—leaves, leaves, leaves. Season after season we have waited patiently for its snow-white blossoms to set fruit. Few, few ever did. Last summer only a few** small handfuls of stunted fruit came off this imposing tree. And this year there will be almost none to even taste. But leaves, leaves, leaves are everywhere. In quiet, pensive moments, working in the deep shade of that spreading, green-leafed tree, I have come to understand clearly what Christ meant when He uttered the simple words, 'For the tree is known by his fruit!' Not by its appearance, not by its imposing size, not by its vigorous growth, and not by its abundance of leaves, leaves, leaves. Instead, the Master Gardener comes looking for fruit. The sweet fruit of His own character, His own conduct, and His own consecration made real in me!"

Just recently I learned of this hymn from Mrs. H. S. Lehman. *"The Master is seeking a harvest in lives He redeemed by His blood; He seeks for the fruit of the Spirit, and works that will glorify God. Nothing but leaves for the Master, Oh, how His loving heart grieves. When instead of the fruit He is seeking, we offer Him nothing but leaves!"*

AN ESCAPE FROM NAZARETH

MARK 1:35 ... HE went out, and departed into a solitary place.

If Jesus needed at times to escape when he was an adult, don't you think he needed to escape from Nazareth? Sometimes I need to escape. Sometimes I feel the city has made me a prisoner. Surrounded by the houses and the businesses of this small coastal city of Ellsworth, I get closed in both in body as well as in mind. Sometimes I need to simply run away to the country where my surroundings are open and my eye sees nothing of mankind or his maddening walls. I felt like that when I lived on the family farm in Perham, Maine. I'd get a bad bout of cabin fever, but even in the worst of weather I got out and about. Did Jesus?

Yesterday I strolled away from the farm house I called home to climb a hilltop that has always cast its shadow over the barnyard. I use to escape to that hill and its woody slopes whenever I could. The moment I would start climbing I would enter another world, a world void of family or friends, a world without man's devices and deadlines. No matter how the farm changed from year to year, that hill and its surrounding forest stayed the same. When one escapes to that hilltop, one moves into the realm of the unchanging. The birds on that hilltop never learned a new song because the old ones were good enough. The wild flowers that bloomed in spring along the roadside never changed color because they were already painted with the best colors. The sky over that hilltop was either a clear day blue, a dark day gray, or a sun setting red. The modern colors have yet to invade the prism of colors cast at God's original creation.

I have always found great peace in slipping into something that stays unspoiled, just like it was, is, and will be. Perhaps, that is why I wear the same style of clothes, part my hair the same way, and enjoy going back to the same fishing hole year after year. When I escape, whether then or now,

AN ESCAPE FROM NAZARETH

I want to escape to the familiar. I seek no new vision or vista. I find great comfort in the same-old-thing. But sometimes in the bedlam of the broadway, I forget that there is such a world still out there. I have been captured by a society that cares little for the sanity of the soul. Granted, to move from one world to the other, to escape from here to there, can be a shock to the system, but it is worth the chance of a heart attack each time.

We have almost lost the ability to escape in this world of constant motion. To walk and meditate is a lost art, and the woods and hilltops that once brought us great relief have been covered over with housing developments and strip malls. As I plan my next escape, I take great solace in the fact that Jesus also had to find a solitary place or two to survive his early pilgrimage. I believe Jesus learned in Nazareth how to escape, but he also knew as we do that we always must return to "another day in Nazareth."

PATIENCE IN NAZARETH

LUKE 21:19 IN YOUR patience possess ye your souls.

As I write "Another Day in Nazareth," it is late March, and I have yet to start my walks along the Union River. Late last fall, I walked almost daily as autumn's best was everywhere, but with everywhere also appeared the onset of the year's darkest season. As the leaves floated down before my eyes, I was reminded that I was going to have to be patient for the return of spring. Jesus never asks us to practice anything He Himself hadn't lived. (Hebrews 4:15) I believe He practiced the precept printed above in Nazareth.

For me and many others, the best part of winter is that it comes just before the glorious advent of nature's restoration, those few wonderful weeks which are so long in coming and so swift in departing. It is worth the wait, and it is worth the winter. I learned early that waiting wasn't bad if you had something worth waiting for. There were plenty of things worth being patient for on the family farm in northern Maine. I loved waiting for the first day when it felt like spring. A day when you could take off your heavy winter coats, if only for a few hours, and play toss with your best friend while you talked about opening season for the Perham Pirates (our baseball team). I loved waiting for the first sound of a robin sounding the "all clear" to the other birds who vacationed in Maine in the summer. It was a sight worth waiting for to watch a robin stroll across the newly cleared lawn in search of spring's first worm.

The birth of a new Holstein calf was worth waiting for. I can still remember the sight and sound and pure delight of watching the young calf struggle to its feet, take its first steps, feed its first meal, and then watch it play with the other calves that had been born. Spring was birthing time on the Blackstone homestead, and that was certainly worth waiting for. I also remember waiting for that first tractor ride in the spring. All winter the tractors and trucks were stored away in the tool shed. About the only piece of equipment that gets much use in the winter was the tractor with the snow scoop on front. With the onset of spring the farm equipment was pulled from storage and worked on. Oil had to be changed, grease had to be applied, and tanks had to be filled. Then each piece had to be tested. There was nothing sweeter to a farm boy then traveling down a field road with spring air in your face and a Deere (John Deere tractor) under your seat!

Sometimes waiting breeds impatience, but when you know the end is near and the smells, sounds, and starts of spring are right around the corner, then waiting isn't that bad because with the coming of winter the next season has to be spring. As a favorite author once put it, **"But winter must come and spring has never failed to follow!"** Jesus taught us patience through his long stay through Nazareth's seasons.

NIGHT IN NAZARETH

PSALMS 22:2 ... IN the night season ...

Have you ever walked out into a night when the sky was cloudless and moonless? Did Jesus in Nazareth?

I live in a city now where the bright lights of downtown can be seen for miles. Such brightness will block much of the glory of a night sky. To really see the glory of a star-studded sky, you have to get away from any natural or artificial light. Such a place is my parent's farm in northern Maine. Despite the fact they live only a few miles from a big city (Caribou), the lights of that city are blocked by a hill. On one of those cloudless, moonless nights, the sight is spectacular—as it was in Nazareth.

It wasn't until I studied the sky in school that I was taught that there are at least 250,000,000 x 250,000,000 stars. (And to think that Jesus knew them each by name and number-Psalms 147:4) Probably with the new giant telescope in space even that number has been increased. The number of stars we can see is small compared to the number of stars we can't see. The night sky really takes on a new meaning and understanding when we realize that most stars, if not all, are larger than our own sun. (Feel small yet?) I was told once that even if we could transport our most powerful telescope to our nearest neighboring star, Alpha Centauri, and set its point back towards planet earth, it would be impossible to make out our 'blue marble' world.

Long before television invaded Perham, the Blackstones would spend many an evening on the front porch. Along with the light show from above there was the light show from the bugs in the field across the road. In the dark, it appeared that there was just as many tiny lights in the tall hay field as there were in the night sky. It is still amazing to me to consider the two extremes of the night. On the one hand it appeared that one could reach up

NIGHT IN NAZARETH

and grab a fist full of stars, and then on the other hand one had such a hard time stooping down and picking up a handful of lightning bugs. The nights of Perham certainly contained a lot of humbling.

Besides the light shows in a homestead night, there were also the sound shows. When the stars and bugs came out, so did the night sounds. Whether the distant moos of the cows in the pasture behind the barn or the occasional bark of my dog Rover as he reacted to an unfamiliar noise, the night was filled with sounds. The final choir of birds could be heard practicing in the forest across Route 228. The frogs could be heard voicing their opinion of the night air in the ponds around the barnyard. From the porch you could also hear the McDougal children (our neighbors up the road) playing in their front yard. Behind them the night sounds of the forest insects would filter down towards us. Night on the homestead never drove us inside, and I wonder now if the same was not true of Jesus in the night season in Nazareth.

CONTENT IN NAZARETH

PHILIPPIANS 4:11 . . . FOR I have learned, in whatsoever state I am, therewith to be content.

If Paul learned it, don't you think Jesus practiced it in Nazareth?

I remember being content as a child. (I even think my parents would agree with me.) I believe the reason I was content was the great parents I had. They provided a warm meal, a warm bed, and warm clothes. Basic human needs were provided in a loving, caring place. Granted, there was more to be had, but what I didn't know I didn't need. Even to this day I am discovering there is another world out there with products and places I have never wanted because I never knew they existed. Perham was a much closed place when I was young, and the homestead was basically the entire world I knew and, now I see, needed. I was content because I was cared for, and my life was managed by loving people. The same with Jesus.

When I say I didn't want for anything, I mean I didn't lack anything. Granted, we didn't have a television until I was nearly a teenager, but as I have discovered, I really didn't need a television. We didn't have all the modern gadgets, and most jobs were done by hand, but in an attempt to make life easier, mankind has actually made life more complicated. Ours was simple, straightforward existence with plenty of food, a comfortable house, and plenty of work to fill our days. We didn't have a lot of time for pleasure and parties, but I have discovered pleasure and parties are not where contentment is found. To grasp the inner significance of this simple statement, it is necessary to understand the difference between "wish" and "want."

What we wish for isn't necessarily what we need, or want. I too was tempted on occasion to wish I was somewhere else, but ever since I got to somewhere else I have wished to go back. Sometimes I wished I was somebody else's child, but ever since I have become somebody else's, I am thankful I still have the same mother and father. Sometimes I wished I had more of the world possessions, but now I wish I had less. With more comes more responsibility and liability. As I have grown older I have come to realize that my parents were the best of parents. They met my needs, not my wishes, and in doing so taught me the greatest lesson of all, that being happy isn't attained by getting everything you wish for. It is attained by being content with what you have. Sometimes I would look over the fence to what I thought were greener pastures, but as I look back now, I realize the grass was greenest on my side of the fence in Perham.

Contentment is more a state of mind than your state. Jesus practiced contentment in a small town for thirty years, and I too have come to understand that sometimes in "another day in Nazareth" you need to learn and practice contentment.

THE PHILOSOPHY OF NAZARETH

Colossian 2:8 ... philosophy ...

I was not raised in a college town, but the town I was raised in gave me a great education. I was not taught by the scholarly, but by men and women of the soil. I can see now that my hometown of Perham did have a philosophy, and that philosophy has after all these years become my philosophy. I have come to believe that philosophy was also in Nazareth.

As the farmers of Perham planted crops of potatoes, oats, and peas, they also planted the precious seeds of common sense and practical living in the well prepared fields of another generation. As they hedged us in and husbanded us, they also looked with great hope towards the harvest. As they labored among the pasture lands and woodlands of their individual farms, they also worked in our lives to instill in us the "Perham Philosophy." Crops don't just miraculously spring out of the ground and neither did likable offspring. Strong and healthy crops don't just flourish by whim or accident, and neither did good kids. Hard work, long hours, and the right kind of weather were all requirements for a successful season, and many hours and even more patience was required to produce a successful son or daughter. But now I see the people of Perham and especially my family on the farm had a plan, a philosophy.

I see now that we the children of that countryside community were the real gardens, real fields, and real pastures of our parents and neighbors. Most of the fields of Perham are returning to the forest they started from, but the kids of Perham, scattered all over the world, are still producing. When the last potato harvest in Perham is over, the harvest of people will continue on. The fragrant fruit of well cultivated character will live on through the "Perham Philosophy." Oh, there has been many disappointments, as there was in the harvests of the past when no fruitage was found or the crop was sparse and sickly, shriveled and shrunken. Land or lad, there has always been a wild weed, a fickle flower, or a vexing vine or two in the field, even in Perham, Maine, or Nazareth.

So what was the "Perham Philosophy?" It wasn't just one creed or one belief. It was a series of lifestyle instructions that had been developed over a hundred years of living by many generations of Blackstones and the other families of Perham. The "Perham Philosophy" had to be learned by living in Perham and watching how the people of Perham lived. Perham people were not tellers, but doers. The "Perham Philosophy" wasn't delivered in a lecture, but shared by a life. Being a visual learner by my very nature, this was the perfect place for me to live and grow. I saw this philosophy lived out before me on a daily basis, and though it took a while to accept it, I believe now I understand it, in summary, as "another day in Nazareth.

THORNS IN NAZARETH

JOHN 19:2 AND THE soldiers platted a crown of thorns . . .

Knowing what Jesus knew, what do you think his first thought was when he encountered his first thorns in Nazareth? I am no expert on thorns and thistles, but I had many an encounter with them on my father's farm in Perham, Maine.

I can't say our farm was totally infested with weeds, but we had our share of noxious plants. Because of where our homestead was located, the topography and terrain was well suited to briers and brambles. Ever since the curse on Adam, farmers have had to do battle with undesirable thorns and thistles that despite spraying and plucking always return year after year to even the best kept ground. I can still see the weed we called 'mustard' invading our oat fields. I have seen my dad and Gramp stop their car or pickup along the road and get out in their Sunday-go-to-meeting suit to pick a clump of mustard they had just noticed. I still remember the long hours in the hot sun with my cousins going row by row through the potato field to pick a weed we called "barn grass." My farmer parents didn't want any competition in their fields. Once a weed was spotted, that weed was removed without any mercy or thought.

The reason that thorns, thistles, briers, and brambles were such a threat was their ability to produce more rapidly than the oats or potatoes we grew. A field choked with mustard and barn grass would smother or stifle the native plants. I can still hear my grandfather say as we travelled beside a neighbor's field overrun with mustard, **"That is the only crop he will get this year."** Gramp was into producing grain and spuds on his land not mustard, and even despite the best efforts of my grandfather, an absolutely clean cultivation of our land was impossible. Weed seeds were always being blown in by the winds from neighboring fields, and bird's dung would deposit weed seeds in their droppings. Even wild animals could carry all sorts of burrs and briers on their coats and deposit them on the homestead. Gramp and Dad knew they would never ultimately win the battle, but with my help they kept up the fight against the plant that bites.

I wasn't very old before I too had gotten a taste for the battle with the brier and the tussle with the thorn. Once I learned what to look for, I too was plucking and picking whenever I saw a strange head in the garden or field. Constant diligence is the best defense against the weed. Did Jesus pick weeds or try to destroy the thorns. Did he ponder the place thorns would have in his future? A crown of thorns would eventually be placed on the head of Jesus from Nazareth as a diadem of suffering. The first time a thorn pricked his finger; did he imagine the pain this cursed plant would bring to his brow? The thistles of Nazareth were just a forewarning of the thorns of Calvary.

THE WILDFLOWERS OF NAZARETH

PSALMS 103:15 . . . AS a flower of the field . . .

As I approach my sixtieth spiritual birthday, I am amazed at the memories I have of the old homestead of my youth and what Jesus must have experienced. The sights and sounds of that time are more precious to me now than they were then. I took for granted the wonderful experience I had as a barnyard boy, but only now do I realize that they were fleeting and temporary at best. The best part of my life I rushed through wanting to grow up and get out. Today, as I remember "another day in Nazareth," my mind floats back to a time in the spring when the wildflowers began to appear along the lanes of the farm as they must have appeared in Nazareth.

As I continued my work in the warmth of a spring sun, I noticed for the first time the wildflowers along the side of Salmon Lake Road. I wish I could name them as Jesus did, but I only knew them as wildflowers. I never cared to learn their exact names, much like the birds and the trees. I do remember on occasion picking a bouquet for Mother. She loved and still loves flowers. It seemed on this day nature was in full bloom with the wildflowers of northern Maine. Not only along the road, but also in the cow pasture the delicate flowers of early spring were beginning to appear among the grazing Holsteins. The land was green enough to release the cows from their winter prison in the barn so as they ate the first green grass of the year, they did it among springing flowers. Did Jesus see such sights as well?

Not only were the wildflowers dancing in a fresh spring breeze, but for the first time in months, the young and old cows were getting into the joyfulness of their first day in the open fields. It was almost laughable as the cows began to run and frolic in the grass. One by one they realized they were free from harness and stall. It was now their option to roam and feed at will. So there in the midst of wildflowers was a herd of cows dancing to the tune of spring, and I danced, too.

Leaving the pasture, I walked up through the Sugar Woods. As with the open field the narrow band of land between road and woods was bursting forth with wildflowers. There were big ones and small ones seemingly of every color of the rainbow. Their tiny bodies lined the wetlands along the road. Land where the water from the snow had melted had created small watersheds that gave enough moisture for the tender plants to grow. As I walked along the nearly quarter mile of highway through my favorite section of the homestead, the wildflowers greeted me in yellow, pink, red, and violet. The scenery, as far as you could see, was beyond proper description. Perhaps that was the way it was supposed to be because the return trip to a time long ago when wildflowers highlighted and underlined a morning walk can only really be experienced in the mind of Jesus when he proclaimed, "Consider the lilies of the filed . . . " (Matthew 6:28)

THE COUNTRY OF NAZARETH

JOHN 4:44 FOR JESUS Himself testified, that a prophet hath no honour in His own country.

    I have lived in Maine most of my life, but I have lived away as well. I believe that one can only have a true opinion if they have experienced both aspects of living here and living there. Most people grow up in Maine only to leave and find their Maine somewhere else. There are those who are born away, but choose to move to Maine and call it home. And then there are those like me who were born and raised in Maine and were called away for one reason or the other, but realized that "Maine was where it was at" and moved back to live. It took some of us moving away to discover that only in Maine is "life as it ought to be." Now that you understand my feelings about Maine, maybe, just maybe, you can understand what Jesus meant when he testified of "His own country."

    My family's roots are in the northern county of Maine. In 1861 my great-great-great grandfather created a farm out of virgin wilderness north of the Aroostook River. I am one of a sixth generation to be born on that homestead, and for twenty-two years I called it home. I left in 1969 to attend college in South Carolina. I returned to marry only to leave again for a pioneer work in New Hampshire. Five years later I returned, but my stay only lasted eight years. At the writing of this memory, I have been away thirty-two years, but I haven't lost my love for the country of my birth. Did Jesus?

    Sometimes when I return for a visit, I climb again into the haymow of the old barn that was built in 1930. On a pile of hay I create a mourner's bench. As I look around the stately barn and allow the memories to flood back, a tear comes to my heart if not to my eye. The changes that have taken place are sad to me. I know why there are no more dairy cows, and I know why there are no more planting of potatoes, and I know why the woods have been cut over, but my sadness changes very little. I am a relic of an age long passed, and I know it because my country is a relic long passed. It was created for potato farms and dairy farms and both are no longer money-making enterprises. Aroostook County did well in a small world with little communication and even less technology. The hearty people that lived there could adapt and be content with the seasons and the weather and the climate. As with Jesus, I too tried to go back to the town of my childhood, but was rejected as their pastor.

I don't know how long it will take or if it will ever happen, but this I know. If possible I would love to be an Aroostook country boy again. To once again, even for a short time, live in the country of my boyhood, to travel full circle and return to where I started, and to experience once more the country freedom and celestial quietness and crossroad living of my idyllic past. Jesus did. Will I?

(A wonderful footnote to this memory of Perham is the fact at the publishing of this book a major change has happened to my family's farm. Most of it has been sold, including my seven acres, to people who are turning the farm back 100 years. A group of Amish people are now farming this land, and though the potatoes are not back, the cows are. I might never return, but when I do return, I see the farm only again as it once was. When Jesus returns to this earth, will one of his first stops be back to Nazareth?)

A JAUNT THROUGH NAZARETH

LUKE 2:39, 40 . . . they returned into Galilee, to their own city of Nazareth. And the child grew, and waxed strong in spirit, filled with wisdom: and the grace of God was upon Him.

As a boy, an afternoon jaunt through the cow pasture was an adventure worth remembering. Did Jesus take afternoon jaunts through Nazareth as he grew and waxed strong?

Just before milking time, I would find a walking stick and head across the Russell Place pasture to get the Holstein herd near the Sugar Woods. I would leave the milking shed through the back door as Dad got the milking machines ready in the front part of the old shed. It was my job to gather the herd for milking, but it wasn't really a job to me.

I headed down through the gully that separated the shed from the huge pasture beyond. Wire fence lined each side as I strolled slowly into the tall grass by a small creek that cut the upper section of the pasture in half. Despite the distance, I would start calling, "Here Boss! Here Boss!" Eager to get the last taste of the juicy grass in their stomachs, the white and black cows ignored the "boy."

The summer air was filled with the sweet aroma of clover. The smell was intoxicating and covered up the other smell that a cow pasture could produce. There was also the faint scent of freshly mowed hay from a field just below the pasture. Weather permitting, if the weather held and the dew stayed away, we would be baling that field the next day.

Every time I jaunted through that cow pasture something new and enchanting always showed up. It might be the flock of ravens that haunted the area or a sighting of one of the local groundhogs that inhabited a number of burrows on a knoll overlooking the small watering pond. On this afternoon it was a flash of red as I watched a mother fox heading back to

A JAUNT THROUGH NAZARETH

her den with a field mouse in her mouth. "Her baby pups would be having supper tonight," I thought to myself.

Despite the growth of the season, the cows had carved paths with their hooves in the ground. Creatures of habit, they seemed to follow similar lanes to the rich feeding ground on the backside of the pasture. Following those trails eventually brought me to the purpose of my jaunt. Knowing the reason for my arrival, the cows immediately stopped feasting and started heading for the milking shed. At first I thought it was my provoking them that started the herd moving, but I learned in time it was the rich grain waiting for them when they got into their stalls. Frequently along the way back, I might have to poke a cow who found a sweet patch of clover. A few taps of my walking stick usually did the trick, and by the time we climbed the small rise to the shed on the knoll, all the milkers were present and accounted for.

I imagine Jesus took similar walks through Nazareth. Whether carpentry or cattle, boyhood jaunts helps one grow.

A REMEMBRANCE OF NAZARETH

Acts 22:8 ... And He said unto me, I am Jesus of Nazareth ...

    A forest of tall maples bordered the winding road leading to the old homestead house and barn. Laden with a late winter ice, the trees and bushes of the Sugar Woods stand as ice sculptures along the lane. Tiny droplets of water sparkle like multicolored rainbows as the warming rays of the morning sun melts nature's masterpiece.

    It is a pretty reminiscence into my past as I revisit the farm of my boyhood in my memory. I walk again that treasured path until I stand exposed to the elements on a small knoll overlooking this picturesque scene. To follow the road is the wish choice, but I choose a detour through the open field along the fence line and tree line. The barnyard before me is a landscape of white and green. The evergreens stand out against the brilliant white of a new snow. This barren field is dotted by a few small patches of barren bushes just waiting the first sign of spring. As I plod through the knee-deep snow, I take in the panorama before me. There to my left is the top of a cedar post just visible in the snow drift near the trees. Before me is the recognizable dent that reminds me of the small pond that is there. Covered in snow and ice, the small stream and pond won't appear again until the robins return.

    As I make my way slowly along the fence line, I observe the cow barn as it grows tall before me. I am walking up to the back of the barn where a single window and a single door are located. The window gives you a view from the first floor into the pasture behind the barn. In the summertime I watch for ravens from that window, but now it is closed against the harsh weather of winter. The door leads to the cows in the basement of the massive barn. It is through that door that all the manure is hauled by wheelbarrow. I will be at that work before my day is through, but as for now, I continue my walk around the barn to my home.

As I stand under the shadow of the old barn, I look up into its dizzying height. It is the tallest structure, manmade or heaven-made, in the barnyard. On warm summer days I climb the rusty, old, iron ladder to the top to catch a cooler puff of wind. Today I will stay on the ground and dream of warmer breezes and summer climbs. It is then my daydreaming is interrupted by the barking of a dog and the wagging of a tail. Rover has heard me coming out from behind the barn and has joined me in the final fifty yards of my trek through forest and field, snow and ice.

When Jesus from heaven introduced Himself to Saul on the road to Damascus, He said, "I am Jesus of Nazareth." Does Jesus from His throne next to the Father remember "another day in Nazareth" on occasion as I have remembered another day in Perham today? I have come to believe that Nazareth still holds a dear place in the heart of God's Son.

THE CROSSROAD OF NAZARETH

JOHN 1:45 ... JESUS of Nazareth ...

When I was just a lad I lived on a crossroad. Not a four-way crossroad, but a three-way crossroad. As we have mentioned before, Nazareth was a crossroad town as well.

For a large part of the year my crossroad was banked in snow. Sometimes the roads that led to my crossroad were closed because of heavy snow. At other times they were icy and dangerous, but just right for sliding because one of the roads to my crossroad went up a very steep hill heading for Caribou. When the traffic was shut off, the crossroad became the best sliding track in the State of Maine.

My favorite time of the year on the crossroad of my family's farm was autumn. It was then the crossroad from Perham to Caribou to Tangle Ridge was alive with color. On two corners of this crossroad were fields. One was a hay field that had already yielded its plenty of green grass, but by fall was a pasture to the young herd growing strong through a wonderful summer. The third corner was now ablaze in yellows, reds, and oranges as the maples, oak, and pine were transformed into a rainbow of colors. In my opinion there is still nothing better than to stand on that crossroad when autumn gets dressed up in its fall finest.

Then there is a country spring on the crossroad. Next to fall my favorite time of the year is spring. With the snow banks melting and the sun growing in strength, the crossroad on Route 228 takes on an entirely different appearance. Wildflowers can be seen along the roadsides. Grass begins to grow next to the road because there are no breakdown lanes on 228. Water flows in the ditches, and wildlife can be seen in abundance. Standing at the crossroad, looking down its roads and pondering what might be at the end, caused a young heart to daydream of far off and distant places. I

THE CROSSROAD OF NAZARETH

remember as a boy wondering what was beyond my crossroad and which direction I would eventually take. Would it be to the city of Caribou, or to the town of Washburn, or would I live the rest of my life in Perham? Jesus, however, knew His route.

When summer came to the crossroad on the homestead, it became a place of traffic. Whether loads of hay or loads of manure, I would cross and re-cross that crossroad hundreds of times in the months of June, July, and August. School was out and plenty of farm work needed to get done before the next blast of winter came roaring through the Sugar Woods. It was a crossroad you never stopped at unless giving a right of way. It allowed you the freedom to exit and enter every part of the homestead. It was the junction of our summer life.

Jesus also passed through the seasons of his Nazarene life at a crossroad of cultures, commodities and climates. Through his life, from birth to death and thereafter, he could never shake the name, Jesus of Nazareth. No matter the direction he went, he was always known as Jesus of Nazareth.

A PATH IN NAZARETH

MATTHEW 3:3 ... PREPARE ye the way of the Lord, make His paths straight.

By now you know I love to walk. Walking requires only one thing—a path. Nazareth was one of the paths Jesus had to walk during his early pilgrimage, and John the Baptist his cousin knew it.

Paths can be marked as was the snow path to the old potato house behind my homestead home. When winter got serious in Perham, the snow banks got high and the going got tough. Dad only plowed half our circle driveway in the winter so to get to the potato house to check the spuds or to start a fire, which we did on the coldest nights; a path through the snow drifts had to be made. That path would be visible until the next wind, when, like the rest of the marks on the snow pack, it would be wiped clean by a gusty gale.

Paths can be secret, as I remember an old boyish path between my neighbor's home and the old stand of building across from my childhood house. Created by the feet of young people playing childish games, this path was through woods of fir, spruce, and pine. The forest canopy was thick making the path dark and spooky at times. Along the path there were great places to hide during Cowboys and Indians. The path was also a pleasant place to get alone when alone was on your heart and mind. Did Jesus have a secret path?

Paths can be private. I am reminiscing on this in the beginning of my sixty-seventh spring. My wife, then only a new found girlfriend, and I use to walk a certain path when she would come to the homestead for a visit. It was the spring of '69 and the wildflowers along our walking path were nothing short of beautiful. A new love is like a walk on a country path—fresh, fun, and full of sun-drenched blossoms. Hand in hand the path leads you to a new world of companionship.

A PATH IN NAZARETH

Despite the many paths I walked on the family farm, the one that brings the most memories were the cow paths. Being raised on a working dairy farm, the landscape throughout the open fields revealed cow paths. Our Holstein herd was free to roam over a large part of the farm. Pasture land and meadows made up a majority of the land. Don't get me wrong, they were fenced in, at least most of the time, but cows tend to be follow-the-leader types. Where one went, the herd went, and it wasn't long before a path was created. Walking a cow path contains a number of dangers, but a "cow-boy" must tread those paths to get the milkers to the milking shed for milking time. One must be careful of dung and exposed rocks. On numerous occasions I stumbled and fell coming face to face with a pile of cow manure. It is on such trails of life you learn to walk cautiously and carefully. I learned many things on the paths of my youth and so did Jesus. Country paths aren't always easy, but the best thing they have going for them is that they are in the country, like "another day in Nazareth."

A DAWN IN NAZARETH

JOB 3:9 ... THE dawning of the day.

    A few days ago I got up before dawn to head for a favorite fishing hole in Washington County, Maine. From my home in Ellsworth I travelled through the dawning morning to get ahead of any other fishermen that might be heading to Grand Lake Stream. As I travelled the hundred miles to that fabled landlocked salmon brook, I pondered a similar dawn on the family farm in northern Maine and in Jesus' Nazareth.

    It was not fishing that got me up early back in my boyhood days, but milking. Being raised on a dairy farm, a dawning dawn always found a couple of the Blackstone boys milking. A hint of red in the predawn sky could be seen either from the back door of the main cow barn or from the back door of the milking shed overlooking the dale. Forest covered hills surrounded the cow pasture as the colors of dawn slowly got bright. As more light made its way over the horizon to the east, the top of the sun could be seen in the distance struggling to make its way up and over the hills toward Caribou. As the reddish ball finally made its way into the sky, the early morning stars that were still up when I got up suddenly winked for the final time and disappeared. Dawn had come to the Blackstone homestead.

    The mooing of the cows brought me back to the task at hand. Despite the beginning of the dawn, the chores still were not done. There were oats to be distributed, eggs to be collected, and milk to be carried. It seemed as soon as one chicken cock-a-doodle-dooed, they all took up the chant until you fed and watered them. It seemed to be the same with the cows. As soon as one moo echoed off the side hill, a score or two could be heard in the valley calling for their special scoop of grain. They sought their food more then they sought your attention. I paid attention, but not to the chickens or the cows. My affection on those early dawns was for a collie/German mix

A DAWN IN NAZARETH

called Rover. Rover was a "dawn" dog without question. Rare would be the morning that he didn't beat everybody up. With a wagging tail and sharp bark to say "Good Morning," Rover would be my companion during my early morning routine.

The fresh morning air would only make the dawn that much fresher. It was a new day, a new start, and a new opportunity to finish the haying or the planning or the mending of the potato house roof. Chores that ended at dark without getting finished would be picked up again at dawn. It might be plowing the back forty if this dawn came in late autumn. It might be finishing loading a trailer of potatoes for market if this dawn came in late January. Whatever the time of year, the only elements that changed the timing of our homestead dawn was the season and the weather. Early or late, it always came. Sun drenched or cloud covered, it always broke through the overcast to start our "Nazareth" morning.

BOYHOOD IN NAZARETH

LUKE 2:51, 52 AND He went down with them, and came to Nazareth . . . And Jesus increased in wisdom and stature, and in favor with God and man.

I have concluded that after over a half century that one's youth was not a time of one's life, but a state of one's mind. It was not carefree days and back lane walks, but a period of imagination and experience. It was not a fairy tale, but it verges on the edge of fantasy and myth.

When I was a youth on my parent's farm in northern Maine, mine was a life of courage, not timidity. I didn't fear man, beast (except the Holstein), heights, or hard work. Mine was an appetite for adventure, not a life of ease. These attributes are often found in children rather than adults. They exist in a lad of twelve verses a man of fifty. The older we get the more we hold back, but a boy in his youth never holds back because he sees no danger and thinks no harm will ever come to him, no matter what.

Someone has written, **"Nobody grows old merely living a number of years; people grow old only by deserting their ideals. Years wrinkle the skin, but to give up enthusiasm wrinkles the soul. Worry, doubt, self-distrust, fear and despair . . . these are the long, long years that bow the head and turn the growing spirit back to dust."** I have found that to be true in the lives of so many people, and that is why I have tried all my life to keep that youthful enthusiasm, whether in my job or hobby. I am still an enthusiastic preacher and an avid adventurer. Whether fifteen or fifty, there is in every person the love of adventure, the sweet excitement of life, the undaunting challenge that comes with each tomorrow, and the unfailing child-like appetite for what will happen next on this journey we call life.

The same anonymous author of the words above also wrote, **"You are as young as your faith, as old as your doubt; as young as your**

self-confidence, as old as your fear; as young as your hope, as old as your despair." I for one might be feeling a bit older in body these days, but my mind is as fresh as these memories of my youth. I might have aged outwardly, but inwardly I feel as new as the days on the homestead when I would venture out into my world to find what I could find, to explore what I could explore, and to discover what I could discover. There is something about being young on the edge of a wilderness. Only at such times and in such places can one truly sense and see the real beauty that can only be found at such times and in such places. To grow old without making such memories is a sad fate, but I was blessed by both living them and remembering now these times and those places in another day in Nazareth.

We should never forget that as we grow older, like with our youth, *"sunsets are not for sale."* The greatest gifts we have received in life were not bought, but given in boyhood.

BAREFOOT IN NAZARETH

LUKE 22:35 AND HE said unto them, When I sent you without purse, and script, and shoes, lacked you anything? And they said nothing.

I have never been a barefoot kind of guy, but when Jesus asked his disciples about their barefoot days, did he remember times when he too went without shoes?

On my boyhood family farm, I had plenty of opportunities to go barefoot. I also remember others pulling off their boots and bearing all to the elements. My most memorable barefoot story has to do with my two brothers. What is not clear to me at this stage of my life is whether or not I actually witnessed the event, or that it was told to me so many times over the years I thought I was there. Bare feet are remembered most as a summer activity, but my brothers, Jay and Michael, would not let the season stop them from going barefoot. Did Jesus have such stories of his brothers? (Mark 6:3)

As the family tale goes, Jay and Michael were testing each other over who would go get the mail in their bare feet. It was a simple task in the summer when the lawn from the old farm house was covered with soft grass, but what about the dead of winter? The journey from side porch to mailbox was over a concrete deck, down three or four concrete steps, and through a snow pile or two before the icy upward slope of the driveway. We are not talking just feet, but hundreds of feet. We are not talking yards, but many, many yards. The trip normally would take only a few seconds at a normal pace, but in the sub-zero snowy, Maine day, it would be an ordeal—a challenge to say the least.

Because neither brother would back down nor neither brother could talk the other into doing it first, the end result was a race as to who could do it the fastest. The ground rules were very clear. Not only would the brothers

BAREFOOT IN NAZARETH

go barefoot, but in short sleeve shirts and just pants. The goal was to navigate over the slippery surface of the yard with nothing between them and the elements wearing just a typical summer outfit. Were they brave enough and bold enough to do this chore by bearing their soles to the freezing ground outside?

The wind was blowing; adding to the miserable condition outside, and inside there seemed to be no protest from any parents. I can't remember whether or not Mum and Dad were even there. I can't remember seeing my sister Sylvia, but I see in my mind's eye my younger sister Lori. Of course, Lori was daring them on even more then I the big brother. The time was set, the racers were in place, and to defy all, both barefoot brothers completed the task, but who won? I told you my mind isn't clear, but for this "another day in Nazareth" I can't imagine that Jesus didn't have a few barefoot in Nazareth stories to tell His disciples.

DAYBREAK IN NAZARETH

ACTS 20:11 . . . EVEN till break of day . . .

At four in the morning on a cloudless September night, the country air can be crystal clear. The whole world lays sharp, still, and sweet in the silver dawn. The stars blink with an amazing intensity. The moon moves slowly across the dark sky, appearing to droop steadily towards its appointed disappearing act off the western horizon. There is an awesome breathlessness in the Salmon Brook Valley just before daybreak. It is harvest time on the Blackstone homestead, but before the potatoes can be dug the cows have to be fed and milked. Did Jesus experience such daybreaks?

These are those sacred, special times I remember most as I think back on my past. Those quiet hours I spent with my dad in the colors of early fall. The multi-colored leaves of autumn would soon be a distant image in my mind, but on this pre-dawn trip to the milking shed there was no sign that the Sugar Woods would not always be draped in orange, crimson, and gold. The wind was somewhere else, and nothing stirred. There were no bending branches, no tumbling leave. For one divine moment the world was at perfect peace with itself and a farm boy from Perham.

On daybreaks like this there is an overpowering sensation that touches your soul in stillness, a quietness so acute that any sound echoes as if off a canyon wall. The waging of a dog's tail is like thunder to your ear, and the moo of a distant Holstein is like a cannon shot. These quiet, morning moments are cherished interludes in the busy schedule of a working teenager. This day would be filled with backbreaking labor, but before the intense work began the good Lord seemed to know that before such a day a delightful daybreak was needed in Perham or Nazareth.

Amid the ebb and flow of the shifting periods of my life, this eternal value has remained. I still cherish my daybreaks, and though they don't

DAYBREAK IN NAZARETH

have to start at four any more, I still enjoy a quiet, gentle beginning to my day. I am one of those that don't have to rush off to a busy office or noisy factory. As I did with my father years ago, I go to work humbled by the breathless beauty of a gathering autumn. Despite the fact I live in a city now, our neighborhood is tree-lined and the sound of a passing car is a couple of blocks away. These city sights and sounds can't rob me of the blinking stars and the setting moon. No man can take away the colorful leaves and the windless morning I step into. My soul is still humbled and I say, **"This is the day the Lord has made. I will rejoice and be glad in it!"** The daybreak is still mine to enjoy.

I still sit alone at times on the church steps and wonder if Jesus took time to enjoy the enchantment of that soft, silver splendor of a golden daybreak in Nazareth as I use to do on my boyhood family farm in Perham.

THE PAGEANTRY OF NAZARETH

JOHN 1:46 . . . CAN there any good thing come out of Nazareth?

I know by now there are those that believe that I have created this place called Perham in my mind, that it is an imaginary place that never existed except in my own memory. That if there was a place called Perham, I have only revealed the best and left out the worst. I grant you; even I sometimes question what I write about. **"Did that really happen, or was that a wishful fantasy of my imagination?"** In some cases, fifty years after the fact, one's memory can get a bit cloudy. Reality sometimes conflicts with fantasy as events fall into clusters of happenings. It is in my opinion called 'the magic of memory'.

I still believe to this day that I was privileged to have been raised in Norman Rockwell's all-American town. We had a general store owned by a man named Max. We had our white-steeple church, and a railroad train ran straight through the town. There was a collection of different colored homes in the village, but the bulk of the residents lived on the side roads leading out of town. The Blackstone homestead could be found about three miles out in the foothills that formed an east to west ridge that ran from Caribou to Ashland. We lived a hardworking, mostly carefree existence, and we did enjoy each other's company when we had a chance to get together. Was this like Jesus' Nazareth?

There were cows, chickens, and pigs on the farm with a few barking dogs and a stray cat or two. There were cousins, aunts, and uncles enough to make a community of our own. We had good neighbors and even better friends. Perham Elementary School was eight grades in four rooms, and our teachers were helpful and friendly. The local pastor came to visit, and nobody locked their doors because there was no crime in Perham. Neighbors helped neighbors in hard times, and a friendly wave was the common gesture of one and all. There was no fear of strangers because there were none.

Having carefully observed the life patterns of the people and places I have lived since Perham, I have come to the conclusion that Perham was a magical place. It was a simple place lost in time and space to a world that decided that such places were no longer needed or necessary for a modern world. The world voted to replace such places with crime cities and a gated community where people live in fear of their neighbors, and strangers are unwanted. Their fast pace is the race to outdo the Joneses rather than help the Joneses, where a wave is a profanity, and a word spoken is an insult. There are no more general stores, and to know your grocer's name is unheard of. The pastor never comes to call, and the local school looks more like a jail then a place of education. Teachers hate their students, and students hate their teachers, and who cares anyway? By now you know that I am convinced that Jesus was also raised in a Perham.

THE LANDSCAPE OF NAZARETH

MATTHEW 4:15 THE LAND of Zabulon, and the land of Nephthalim, by the way of the sea, beyond Jordan, Galilee of the Gentiles.

Foothills are foothills by virtue of the fact that the earth's crust has been wrinkled by the titanic creative force of the Word of God. (Hebrews 11:3) I will not debate with you when the good Lord in His divine providence decided to create the foothills of Nazareth, but to this day I am thankful He did because that meant that Jesus and I were raised in a similar landscape.

Round top hills and rugged hollows cover the town of my upbringing. On those foothills and in those small vales were once found beautiful stands of maple, pine, fir, spruce, poplar, hemlock, and ash. As with any landscape, there is wonderful diversity in Perham. The town has a few small ponds, and then there is Salmon Lake. The landscape is crisscrossed with a number of small creeks, a few streams, and Salmon Brook. No one knows precisely where to stand to view it all, but I do have two favorite spots. Did Jesus have his favorites in his native Nazareth?

The first is on the knoll at FairView Cemetery. From that hallowed spot you can look down into the Salmon Brook Valley. This colorful hollow runs all the way from Salmon Lake to downtown Perham. A plentiful brook trout stream has carved a wonderful valley through a granite lined vale. In autumn the view from the knoll is the best on the planet. I have seen fall foliage all over New England, and the landscape from that observation point has never been duplicated in my humble but prejudiced opinion.

The second is on top of Blackstone Road hill. From cemetery knoll, the land rises one more time until you stand on the highest point of land on the Blackstone homestead. The main buildings and homes of the farm are found just under this hill, and it is a gentle rise to the summit. From the top you have a 360-degree view of the surrounding landscape. Unlike the view from FairView Cemetery which only has a 180-degree view, the circular vista is spectacular any time of the year. From that small foothill you are able to look back into Perham in the valley below. The white steeple of our home church is visible except in fog and snow. Even the distant city of Caribou can be seen most days thirteen miles away. You can see back into the town of Washburn, seven miles in the distance. Whether in the colorful canopy of autumn or the white canopy of winter, the view is without question awe inspiring. The height might not be that of a Mount Washington, but the landscape is unmatched.

The other aspect of this landscape is the fact that man can take no credit for any of this. None of it is of his own making. His pride had nothing to do with the "land" or the "view" because it is all stamped with "made by Jesus." (John 1:3)

THE BIBLE OF NAZARETH

MATTHEW 2:21 AND HE (Joseph) arose, and took the young child (Jesus) and his mother (Mary), and came into the land of Israel (Nazareth).

We live in a world where the value system of most people has gotten way out of focus. We value gold, position, status, and even time itself. My dad has always been one who seemed to understand what real value was all about.

Dad has always believed that God has given us two Bibles, not just one. From my earliest memories I remember seeing Dad's Bible in the bathroom. Being a rocky land farmer all his life, my dad didn't have much time to read the Bible, but he took time. The book of grace was always in front of me, and I was taken to church every Sunday to be taught by it and to listen to it sermonized. But for my dad there was always another Bible he read, the Bible of nature. **"The heavens declare the glory of God; and the firmament showeth His handiwork. Day unto day uttereth speech, and nigh unto night showeth knowledge. There is no speech nor language, where their voice is not heard."** (Psalms 19:1–3) Because Dad spent the bulk of his time in this second Bible, it was from that Word of God he learned and taught about value.

If you think my dad radical and liberal, I would simple point you to Jesus Himself. Sometimes Jesus would preach from a text like in Isaiah (Luke 4:16–32), but at other times He would say, "Behold the fowls of the air: for they sow not, neither do they reap, nor gather into barns; yet your heavenly Father feedeth them. Are ye not much better than they?" (Matthew 6:26) Jesus saw both books as divinely inspired, and so did my dad. Whether a lily or a rose, whether a sparrow or a sower, Jesus taught His disciples and my dad taught me. I have never not believed Job's admonition (Job 12:7–9) because I was taught the value of the lesson from nature as valuable as the lesson from scripture. "Are not five sparrows sold for two farthings, and not one of them is forgotten before God? But the very hairs of your head are all numbered. Fear not therefore; ye are of more value than many sparrows." (Luke 12:6, 7) Granted, if and when they come into conflict, the Bible has preeminence, but in my fifty years as a serious student of the Word of God, I have never found a conflict between the two books, and neither did my dad and neither did Jesus.

The value of this second Word of God has been ignored by the city-society and the town-mentality we live in today. Mankind is afraid of nature (the natural world) because they only see the terror and horror of it. There is a destructive side to the natural world, but there is also the symbolic side. God's value system is not limited to the symbols He uses. There is no flower or fish, no beast or bird, no blade of grass, and no summer meadow that cannot illustrate some divine truth, as the Bible of Nazareth did.

AN ILLUSTRATION FROM NAZARETH

LUKE 2:51 AND HE went down with them, and came to Nazareth, and was subject unto them: but His mother kept all these sayings in her heart.

Though I was taught of the concept of nature as an illustration for so many things in the Sunday school of the Perham Baptist Church and in the Children's Church services of Lily Harris, it was also in the barnyard of the homestead that my dad pointed to Jesus' observations of nature from Nazareth. "And why take thought for raiment? Consider the lilies of the field, how they grow; they toil not, neither do they spin: and yet I say unto you, that even Solomon in all his glory was not arrayed like one of these. Wherefore, if God so clothes the grass of the field, which today is, and tomorrow is cast into the oven, shall He not much more clothe you, O ye of little faith?" (Matthew 6:28–30)

There were few lilies on the farm, but there were plenty of gorgeously robed wildflowers along the highways and hedges. There were no oxen on the farm, but the patience of the ox could also be seen in other farm animals. I was shown the industry of the ant and the skillful hand of the spider. The hind's surefootedness was seen in the fleet foot of the white-tail deer as he bounded away from our watching eye. The speed and majesty of the eagle was rare, but it was there. Whether dove or sparrow or raven or in the case of those who live where the chickadee abides, the birds of the homestead were the most often used example for something when my dad taught his lessons from nature.

They tell me that over forty species of birds are mentioned in the Bible and each is in connection with a lesson or two. Over twenty times a bird's nest is described, and each time some teaching is applied. We had plenty of bird's nests on the homestead. The vast majority could be found in the massive cow barns. I would often climb the rafters to find a bird's nest to see if some egg or chick were still there. Who first pointed out these nests? Dad. He spoke of the wonder of the architecture and construction. He did the same thing when we would come across a beaver dam in one of our walks together. I can still hear him speak of the quality of work these simple creatures performed. Was there a mason, a carpenter, a weaver, or a spinner that could do a better job? With limited resources God's creatures could out-perform most using moss, sticks, grass, and cow's hair. Jesus' point explained!

I watched for years Dad work like the creatures he talked about. Through industry and surefootedness, my dad kept his farm going. His patience still amazes me, and his use of only what was on the land still challenges. His skillful hand was speedy, but sure. I missed it then, but I see it so clearly now because along with the birds and beasts, the flowers and fowl, there was another example before my eyes.

WINGS OVER NAZARETH

PSALMS 91:4 . . . AND under His wings shalt thou trust . . .

To say my dad loves to watch birds would be an understatement to say the least. Dad has been a bird watcher all his life, but over the years I have come to the conclusion that his love affair with fowl and feather has to do with their wings and the meaning of the phrase above.

If one studies the Bible like my dad has, one would find a myriad of references to the wing, both literally and figurative, i.e., "the wings of a dove" (Psalms 68:13), "the wings of the morning" (Psalms 139:9), "the wings of the wind" (Psalms 104:3), "the wings of the Almighty" (Psalms 91:4), "the shadow of His wings" (Psalms 63:7), "the wings of eagles" (Isaiah 40:31), "the wings and feathers of the ostrich" (Job 39:13), and "the Sun of righteousness with healing in His wings" (Malachi 4:2), to name a few. So what was it that drew my dad to the "wing?" I believe this verse in the Bible book of the Psalms, "And I said, oh, that I had wings like a dove! For then would I fly away, and be at rest" (Psalms 55:6) will answer this question.

My dad has always been a man at rest, a man at peace with himself and God. How was it he could lay down after a noon meal and rest a while (15 to 30 minutes) and then instantly return to the field for a hard afternoon of work? Dad found somewhere in his youth to "take the wing of a dove" and fly to a place of rest. His calm nature, even in the midst of crisis, has been a marvel to his family and friends for a lifetime now. Could it be that the very nature of a winged bird rests in the soul of this man? Church history tells me that the great Christian Saint Francis of Assisi once preached a sermon to the birds. All great thinkers have found solace in the presence of the creature created called bird. Some think that they are more a heavenly being then an early creature. Their domain is above, and they seem to take literally Paul's admonition, "Set your affection on things above not on things on the earth." (Colossians 3:2) Jesus also loved watching birds as seen in His sermons.

When Biblical birds take wing they seem to be the bearers of good news. I think of the wings of the ravens that brought Elijah his daily meals (I Kings 17). I am reminded of the wings of the dove that brought Noah the news that the earth was dry enough to leave the ark (Genesis 8). I recall the lesson of Jesus and the protection that can be found under a "chicken's wing." (Matthew 23:37). Who was the first to point these lessons out to me? My dad, the observer of wings and the ways of God. It is no wonder that men like Audubon, Thoreau, and Shelly studied, searched for, and made sonnets to the marvelous flight of the bird, and that the noise of their wings was music to their ears. The reason my father loved birds was his Father loved birds, and so did His Son who was fascinated with "wings over Nazareth."

CARING IN NAZARETH

I Peter 5:7 Casting all your care upon Him: for He careth for you.

I believe one of the first understandings I had about my earthly father was that he cared for me. I saw it from an early age as he took care of my daily needs of housing, food, and clothing. It was never a difficult transition for me when I was introduced to "the care of the heavenly Father.

I was one of the blessed ones to have been given an example of care long before I was confronted with who God was and what I was to do with His Son Jesus Christ. Dad was never much on affection (few hugs and the rare "I love you"), but he was huge on care. I have come to believe that is how my dad shows love and affection. He is the most caring man I have met in my sixty-seven years. I know there are others out there, but next to my grandfather (Dad's Dad), Wendell is the greatest earthly example I know. For years my Grandfather Carroll held that position, but I only was around my grandfather for twenty-four years. Over the years, I have come to see that even Gramp falls into second place behind Dad.

How and when did my dad learn to care? I trace this attribute along with the others back to the time my dad fell into step with his Lord and Saviour Jesus Christ. Dad was a young adult when he made his decision for Christ. It was in those early years he read about the Heavenly Father caring for every sparrow, and that people were more valuable than many sparrows. Long before I was born (1951), my dad was caring about others. He cared for his nation enough to become a soldier, but not just any kind of soldier, but a medic, one who cares for others. He cared enough for his home town to return to it and live and serve it. He cared for the homestead to the point that he returned to it and took care of it throughout the strength of his life. He cared for a wife and eventually a family of five kids, and I have yet to

CARING IN NAZARETH

hear anything said from my two brothers and two sisters that Dad didn't care—no, not once.

Often we get misdirected when we think that God only cares about important events and great people. Why would God care about an unknown in a no account place, yet He does. Jesus came to an unknown place and lived most of his life unrecognized to teach most of us that He cares even for us. The same God that fed the multitudes feeds the single sparrow. My dad was an example of this all his life. My dad hasn't done big or great things, but I stand amazed each time I hear of the little things he did. My dad cared enough to show me that God cares for me in my small unimportant place doing my small unrecognized ministry. The hymn writer asked the question, "Does Jesus Care?" and it was my dad who gave the answer first. "Oh, yes, He cares. I know He cares; His heart is touched with my grief. When days grow weary, the long night dreary, I know my Saviour cares."

CHEERFULNESS IN NAZARETH

MARK 6:50 . . . BE of good cheer: it is I: be not afraid . . .

My dad was a synonym of cheerfulness. I am not saying that my father didn't have days of discouragement or depression. I am not saying that my dad always had a smile on his face and a happy appearance, but what I am saying is that cheerfulness is an attribute that best describes him.

In Perham, Dad's home town, there are winter blizzards to fight through and downpours to contend with, but most days are cheerful. The sun is warm, the breeze is refreshing, and the birds are singing. Such is the case with my dad. Dad speaks with gladness, and the music on his lips is pleasant to the hearer. I have found in most of my encounters with Dad, almost without exception, is cheerfulness. God gave Dad a calm voice, a quiet nature, and a cheerful disposition. Like a calming wind and a warming sun, one feels peaceful around such an individual as I have with Dad. Even on those rare occasions that discipline had to be administered in my boyhood, Dad always seemed to have the situation well in hand, and it was soon forgotten.

Dad taught me by his examples of **"swift to hear, slow to speak, slow to wrath"** (James 1:19) and **"a soft answer turneth away wrath."** (Proverbs 15:1) How did I know that my dad was happy and cheerful? I first saw it in his outward behavior. Dad very rarely got excited or anxious in a crisis. Dad's calmness spoke to me of an inner cheerfulness that balanced itself by a controlled appearance. Then there was the humming. My dad loves to hum, and more often than not it was an old church hymn that he hummed. The calming melody seemed to put my dad in a mellow state. Like the birds singing as they worked so my dad would hum while milking the cows. Some of my earliest remembrances of my father are going into the cow barn next to our home and hearing Dad singing in the basement while mucking out the cows. If you can be cheerful while shoveling manure, then you have found the secret to cheerfulness!

I believe my father had the same opinion about cheerfulness as the great music man Joseph Haydn. One day someone asked the great composer why he always wrote such cheerful music. He replied, **"I cannot do otherwise. When I think of God my soul is so full of joy that the notes leap and dance from my pen."** Dad was never a man to write his thoughts down, but his life has always mirrored the mercy of God on his life, and as Paul wrote, **". . . *he that showeth mercy, with cheerfulness,*"** (Romans 8:9) mercy will result in cheerfulness every time. Father lived his life full of the mercies of God on his life. Just last week as I spent a few days with him and Mother, I saw again his cheerful disposition despite old age, chronic illness, and the sadness that often comes when nearing "the end of the road." I believe Nazareth had such a person living among them for thirty years.

AN EXAMPLE IN NAZARETH

Luke 18:37 they told him that Jesus of Nazareth passeth by.

My father could hardly be called a poet. He was a potato farmer and a dairyman. Throughout his life he was intensely practical. Dad would never burst out with some poetic statement. He is a man that chooses well his words, and when he speaks, he has never been one just to speak for speaking sake. While others never grow weary of talking, Dad waited and wondered and watched until the right moment had arrived for him to speak profoundly. Despite this practical side, Dad also had a very spiritual side. Natural things were to him but images of spiritual things. His entire farm was in tune with God. As somebody put it, **"Tongues in trees, books in running brooks, sermons in stones and good in everything."** Dad was my Nazareth example as Jesus was.

Dad heard the voice of God in the thunder that rolled down through the Salmon Brook Valley. The lightning that flashed over the hills towards Caribou was the glare from God's eyes. The sunshine that flooded the homestead on a warm summer's day was God's smile. No matter the color of the sky or the effect of the weather, the heavens told of the glory of God, and the earth always revealed the handiwork of the Heavenly Father. A man called Ruskin once observed that a Christian should never **"walk over so much as a root of the natural earth without receiving strength and hope from some stone or flower, or leaf or sound, nor without the sense of divine dew falling upon him out of the sky."** My dad lived in that philosophy every day of his life.

To Dad even the most common object about him had a divine message if only our ears and eyes were open to the sermon. We all miss "the wonderful words of life" because of perception or misunderstanding. Ignorance is not bliss when we fail to understand the movement of God in

AN EXAMPLE IN NAZARETH

something around us. This reminds me of a story I read once about the early gold miners in Brazil. As they searched for gold, they would throw away as useless small pebbles found in the vein only to discover later that many of those small pebbles were diamonds. Such is the case with most of us as we travel through this world filled with God's blessings. How many of us have discovered with the passing of time that we too have thrown away many of our best blessings as useless because we were looking for the wrong blessing? The common sailor on Columbus' ship saw the seaweed floating by as just another endless example of the hopelessness of the voyage while Columbus found hope that a new world was near.

Frank M. Goodchild once wrote, **"The greatest men among us are the men who have the power to see things which are directly under the eyes of everybody, but which nobody else sees!"** This is illustrated by the parable of the man who while walking through a forest failed to see any firewood. My dad knew how to spot firewood in every forest he hiked.

WORKMANSHIP IN NAZARETH

EPHESIANS 2:10 FOR WE are His workmanship, created in Christ Jesus unto good works, which God hath before ordained that we should walk in them.

It was my dad that taught me to see God in everything and everywhere. I have always believed that God was a personal Creator that had a hand in every aspect of creation. That is why one of the greatest **"damnable heresies"** (II Peter 2:1) of our day is the abandoning of the idea of divine creation because of the impersonal theory of evolution. Man says, "It rained today." Dad would say, "God sent the rain today." Man says, "The wind is blowing." Dad would say, "God is causing the wind to blow today." Mankind today claims that the earth is running itself, and maybe it fashioned itself some billions upon billions of years ago. Dad saw the glory of God in His workmanship on the farm. Dad believed as I do, **"But the heavens and the earth, which are now, by the same word are kept in store . . ."** (II Peter 3:7) Jesus believed the same thing in Nazareth.

There was a time when man use to see God's workmanship in the earth. But now the geologists who study this planet overlook the signs of God at work. The physicians who explore the workings of the human body, to heal sickness and repair damage done in an accident, no longer see it as God's greatest creation; the astrologers who explore the outer reaches of our solar system no longer look for God, but look for some truth that space is the product of a "big bang." Mankind use to see God in the heavens. The great astronomer, Kepler, while listening to "the story of the stars," is reported to have said, **"O God, I think Thy thoughts after Thee."** Winchell, the great geologist, once said, *"It was God's hand that packed the land together, tossing up the mountains to great heights, and thrusting down the floor of the ocean to great depths."* I am thankful that I was raised by one that believed the same thing as these great men of the past. Dad was not a scholar, nor a scientist, but he still believed in the workmanship of God.

I am convinced that the most important change that is needed in this world today is to bring back God into the midst of all things. How better we would understand the sciences if God was in His proper place. How better we would understand history and would not make the same mistakes of the past if God was back in His key role. How better we would understand the arts if God were once again seen as the Creator of all beauty. My dad believed that God's real name was Emmanuel (Matthew 1:23). If we could but believe again that "**God is with us**," we would see Him again in the "flashing sea," "the amber waves of grain," and the "purple mountains." God was brought down to eye level, not to make Him like us, but that we might see Him as He is, and that we might see that we are His workmanship.

THE SALT OF NAZARETH

MARK 9:50 SALT IS good: but if the salt have lost his saltiness, wherewith will ye season it? Have salt in yourselves, and have peace one with another.

Salt is for seasoning. I remember hearing a story about a king who had three daughters. The king brought them before him one day and asked, "How much do you love me?" The first daughter told her father that she loved him more than all the gold in the world. The second daughter said that she loved her father more than all the silver in the world. The youngest daughter told her father that she loved him more than all the salt in the world to which the king replied that he thought he ought to be compared to something more important than salt. Overhearing the conversation between the king and his three daughters was the royal cook. The next day the cook withheld salt from all the royal meals to the point that the king complained and refused to eat the meals. It was then the royal cook pointed out to the king what the youngest daughter meant when she compared the salt of the earth with her father. She really was saying she loved him so much that nothing was good without him. Life needs seasoning as do people. Is that not why the good Lord called us to be "the salt of the earth" (Matthew 5:13) and has made "a covenant of salt" (Numbers 18:19) with us? Salt would have been an important item in Nazareth.

Salt is for savor. This is why Jesus warns us about losing our savor (Luke 14:34, 35). Our savor is what makes us useful to God. I am convinced this is what Paul feared when he kept his body under subjection (I Corinthians 9:27). He feared the loss of his savor and therefore the loss of his usefulness to God. If I heard anything in Perham, it was the importance of keeping one's testimony as pure as salt. I still can remember hearing in my ear that little instruction as I was tempted to do something wrong. I have told people for years that I survived the teenage years with my testimony

THE SALT OF NAZARETH

intact because of that simple sermon, and I can honestly say to this day that salty truth still keeps me. Are these the same lessons Jesus learned in Nazareth?

Salt is for stealth. Does anyone see what salt does, for the food or the body? No, salt is a secret savor, a silent preservative, a stealth spice. I am convinced this is another reason the Lord called us to be salt. Our influence as a Christian ought to be unobtrusively salty. All that should be seen are the results. Most Christians today are more worried about the credit than the cause. Is not this the way salt works? We do not realize what is being done or that anything is being done. We only know that if it is missing from our food that something is missing. I suspect when Jesus left Nazareth that the people began to realize that something very important was missing from their town—the savor and flavor of their native son was gone.

THE WORLD OF NAZARETH

JOHN 10:36 SAY YE of Him, whom the Father hath sanctified, and sent into the world . . .

Permit me to use this classic church hymn, This is My Father's World, to teach a wonderful concept I learned in Perham that I believe Jesus first sang in Nazareth.

Maltbie Babcock's words speak volumes of what I know. **"This is my Father's world, and to my listening ears, all nature sings, and round me rings the music of the spheres. This is my Father's world, I rest me in the thought of rocks and trees, of skies and seas His hand the wonders wrought."** My Father did create it all, and for me the creator Father made the world of Perham. I was a homebody at best. I travelled little in my first eighteen years in Perham because the world was the rocks and trees, the skies and streams of northern Maine. The Bible says I was created in the image of God, and that He has given me the ability to hear nature sing. I heard it in Perham as Jesus did in Nazareth.

Babcock continues. **"This is my Father's world, the birds their carols raise, the morning light, the lily white declares their Maker's praise. This is my Father's world, He shines in all that's fair; in the rustling grass I hear Him pass, He speaks to me everywhere."** Only man was created with the ability to enjoy nature. The Holstein grazing on the side hill will come across a bunch of daisies growing at its feet, but to the cow that collection of flowers is no more than stubble to be eaten. My earthly father taught me to enjoy the wildflowers, the morning light, and the lily white. I learned to hear God in nature long before I learned to hear Him in the Word of God. Eventually I learned to hear Him everywhere just as we should in every Nazareth.

Babcock concludes. **"This is my Father's world, O let me never forget that though the wrong seems oft so strong, and God is the Ruler yet. This is my Father's world, the battle is not done, Jesus who died shall be satisfied, and earth and heaven be one."** The planet is my Father's world, and the Blackstone homestead was my world as a child, and my dad taught me to acknowledge that God was still its Ruler every day. Dad prayed to God, sought God's advice, and yielded to whatever God sent. The harmony of my Father and my father was the example I needed to show me that ***"this is my Father's world."*** I can easily believe that my heavenly Father delights in contemplating the beauty of nature because my earthly father loves so much contemplating the beauty of nature. This was set in the heart of my father by my Father.

Was not that the example set by Christ as He too made sure that everybody knew **"that I must be about my Father's business?"** (Luke 2:49) If Jesus made that point in Jerusalem, do we not believe He made the same acknowledgement in Nazareth? Jesus wanted everybody to know that Nazareth was His Father's world.

THE CODE OF NAZARETH

ACTS 2:22 . . . JESUS of Nazareth, a man approved of God . . .

Perham's social life revolved around the family in my childhood. Rural families of northern Maine in the 50s and 60s tended to be large, cohesive, and extremely hardworking. The numbers were needed to fulfill the many demands of the farm. The husband of the family was the breadwinner, and the wife was the stay-at-home mother who kept the house and minded the children. Despite the fact that my mother was a college graduate, the moment my older sister arrived she stopped her teaching career to take care of us. It was a social code that was lived by in the back corners of Aroostook County and, could I suggest, a code that would change the decline of the American family today.

The older I get (I just turned 67) the more I realize that my upbringing was much like the upbringing of another young lad many, many years before me. Mine was a Christian family that believed in the teaching and example of Jesus of Nazareth. The moral, religious, and social codes of Nazareth were the moral, religious, and codes of the majority of people of Perham, and especially the Blackstones. Men had serious obligations to their wives (I never, ever saw Dad strike Mum), their children (Dad was always respected), their parents (my father cared for his mother until she reached her 100th year; no nursing home for Gramie), and their community (Dad was always involved in the good of his town). Like with the Nazarene's life, Perham had its immutable rules and established codes to govern one from birth to marriage to parenthood to old age and to death.

I was not very old before I began to see the connection of my life and the life of Jesus. His name was invoked at meal time, and He was talked about as a dear uncle that would soon return after a lengthy absence. I was taken to the local Baptist church regularly to learn more about Jesus of

THE CODE OF NAZARETH

Nazareth. His instructions became my guidelines, and it is not surprising that at the age of seven I accepted Him as my Lord and Saviour. By now you have probably already figured out that nearly sixty years has passed, and I am still living by the code of Christ that was planted in my heart during my years in my Nazareth. Those codes have become my messages for over fifty years now. (I preached my first sermon at the age of fifteen!)

The longer I live the more I come to realize that I have all my life been directed by this simple code that was first established and experienced in the small Galilee village of Nazareth. This code of conduct and character was lived out in the smallest of places so that those of us who would also live in such places could relate, realize, and reason that if the Son of God would do it there, we could do it in our home here. Perham was my Nazareth for 21 years, and the code I left with has carried me through the ministry period of my life, as it did with Jesus.

A SABBATH IN NAZARETH

LUKE 4:16 AND HE came to Nazareth, where He had been brought up: and, as His custom was, He went into the synagogue on the Sabbath day, and stood up for to read.

When I was a kid, our Sabbath day was Sunday instead of Saturday. Despite the fact we believed in the Jewish Jesus, we were Baptist, and we recognized the day of Jesus' resurrection versus the traditional day of rest, the seventh day.

I still remember clearly the differences between the last six days of the week versus the first day of the week. Monday through Saturday was pretty much the same, day after day—working days. My parents and grandparents did believe in the old adage of *"six days shall you labor and do all your work."* (Exodus 20:9) To this day, I still can't break myself of that precept of work no matter how often I try to adapt to the modern philosophy of a five-day or a four-day work week. I still feel guilty when I don't put in a ten to twelve-hour work day for six to seven days a week. I am 67, and I have carried on the work schedule of the farm despite the fact I haven't worked on the homestead for over 45 years. (Footnote: my deacon board at Emmanuel Baptist has just imposed a five-day work week for me; hoping that an extra day a week off will lengthen my ministry among them. Just recently I was talking to a friend who asked if I had retired yet, to which I total him only semi-retired; when I total him semi-retirement ment five-days and 50 hours he only laughed!)

However, when Sunday came, the work did slack just a bit. Because I lived on a dairy farm, we still had plenty of animals that had to be looked after despite the fact it was the Lord's Day. There were early morning chores before Sunday school, and there were late afternoon chores before evening service. My family attended a small Baptist church located in the village of

Perham about three miles from our home. If the doors of the church building were open the Blackstones were there. It was our pattern and routine to attend those services, but it didn't take up the whole day. There was always a few hours in which neither the cows nor the church took our time. It was then my parents taught me about rest. It was important to rest, even when I didn't want to rest. Before television there were games that you could play the other six days of the week, but not on Sunday. There were activities you could participate in the other six days of the week, but not on Sunday.

As I grew older and wiser in the understanding of our faith, I began to realize that what the Blackstones practiced was a Christian form of the Sabbath practices of Mary, Joseph, and Jesus of Nazareth. The only difference that I could see was that Jesus' family lived this way on Saturday, and my family lived this way on Sunday. I went to a church and Jesus went to a synagogue, but we both heard teachings from the Bible. This form of Sabbath day has gone the way of so many traditions of our faith, but I still wonder why. Was there no value in setting aside a time of rest each week? Is there no value in making at least one day a week different then the other days of the week? I for one have a very busy Sunday now that I am a pastor, but I still covet those afternoon naps before my evening chores.

THE BUTTER OF NAZARETH

Isaiah 7:15 Butter and honey shall He eat . . .

Despite the fact I lived on a dairy farm with a huge herd of Holsteins, it was not on that farm I got a taste for real butter. The Blackstone homestead purpose for having dairy cows was milk, not butter. I don't remember seeing much butter being made on the farm, even though I know my ancestors before me did. For me, it was in my friend's mother where I got a taste for cow's butter. It was also in a recent study of the prophetic verse, "Therefore the Lord Himself shall give you a sign: behold, a virgin shall conceive and bear a son, and shall call his name Immanuel" (Isaiah 7:14) that I noticed for the first time the connecting phrase printed above. I realized immediately another direct link between my childhood in Perham and an experience Jesus had in Nazareth. This is what I remember about Perham butter made at the McDougal's house.

First, the cream had to be separated from the whole milk by a hand-turned separator. Milk was first poured into a large container on top of the separator. As the machine was turned, centrifugal force spun the liquid outward. The cream, being lighter, ran out into one pail while the heavier skim milk came out into another pail. There was always more skim milk than cream. The cream, key to making butter, was collected in crocks until enough was gathered to make a batch of butter. Because the McDougal's only had a few cows, it took quite a few milkings, twice a day, to get enough cream to make butter, but once Emma knew she had enough, the butter-making process would begin.

Second, the cream was poured into a wooden butter churn. This too was driven by muscle power. The churning process took place as the handle on the side of the butter churn was turned around and around. I remember being present a few times when this took place. Morris would turn it

THE BUTTER OF NAZARETH

awhile, and then I would take over. Once the cream was churned into a lump, the lump was deposited to a "butter worker" where Emma worked the lump with paddles getting rid of any buttermilk still in the lump. When the lump of butter became firm enough to mold, Emma would sprinkle it with salt, the reason I probably loved real cow's butter so well.

Finally, the lumps of butter were usually shaped into one pound blocks and wrapped in wax paper and put in the refrigerator. All that was needed was something to put the butter on like biscuits or homemade bread. I discovered that different cows made different tasting butter. Unlike the Blackstones who raised only Holsteins, the McDougal's cows varied. It seemed to me their Guernsey cows produced the richest butter, but Jersey butter was also very good. I still prefer the taste of butter over oleo margarine to this day. I have now discovered another link between my childhood in Perham and Jesus' boyhood in Nazareth—butter.

HOME-LIFE IN NAZARETH

MATTHEW 13:55, 56 . . . Is not His mother called Mary? And His brethren, James, and Joses, and Simon, and Judas? And His sisters are they not all with us? . . .

    Like Jesus, I was brought up in the midst of a big family. We are not only told of Jesus' immediate family as seen in the verse printed above, but during Jesus famous trip to Jerusalem at twelve we are told of his **"kinsfolk"** (Luke 2:44). In my childhood in Perham I too was surrounded by aunts, uncles, grandparents, cousins, and **"kinsfolk."**

    Unlike Jesus, I didn't lose my earthly father early in life. (As a matter of fact, my Dad wouldn't travel to heaven until his 93rd year.) Joseph's name disappears from the Bible stories after Jesus turned twelve so Jesus grew to manhood as the older brother. I too know of the older brother title because I have been the older brother since 1961 when my youngest sister, Lori, was born. Is this another reason Jesus was called *"the carpenter"* (Mark 6:3) because he was responsible for the support of his family between the years of his father's death and his ministry?

    It was not until I began to think down this line of thought that I realized that many of Jesus' famous teachings in parable form contained references to home-life, maybe his home-life in Nazareth? What of the story of the woman that turned her home upside down to find a missing coin (Luke 15:8). Who of us hasn't done the same thing over a missing item? Money must have been tight for Mary. Did Jesus come home one day from the carpenter's shop and find his mother searching? What of the measure of flour and leaven in the baking of bread (Matthew 13:33). How often did Jesus witness his mother making the weekly bread do the same thing? My mother made bread every Saturday so I too watched the process unfold. What of the plight of the man who found the cupboard bare at the arrival

HOME-LIFE IN NAZARETH

of an unexpected guest and his visit to a neighbor to borrow some bread (Luke 11:5). Did Jesus have a similar experience in Nazareth? We could speak of lighting candles (Matthew 5:15), children coming home after school or play for a snack (Matthew 7:9), and countless other home-life events that Jesus witnessed in Nazareth and would later use in his parables to teach us godly lessons.

Life in Mary's house became the backdrop of many a future sermon, and I have discovered after 45 years in the pastorate that I too use similar experiences from my time in Perham to illustrate points in my messages. I like Jesus have discovered a wealth of stores and illustrations in my memory bank that fit perfectly the concept I am trying to get across to my congregation. Life in a small town and with a large family contains the examples I often need to help my students understand a divine truth. Jesus used his home-life in Nazareth to proclaim his truth, and I have done the same with my experiences in Perham, Maine, in the 50s and 60s.

A NAZARENE IN NAZARETH

MATTHEW 2:23 . . . HE shall be called a Nazarene.

One thing I quickly learned from my Bible at the Perham Baptist Church in my boyhood was that Jesus had many names. This truth only grew in magnitude as I read and studied the scriptures more and more. Warren Wiersbe once said, **"Every name that He wears is a blessing that He shares."** I am coming to believe the deeper I get into this parallel between Jesus' days in Nazareth and my days in Perham that Nazarene was one of Jesus' most coveted names.

I have become very proud of being called a **"Maineaic,"** a resident of Maine. I know that for some it is a name that speaks of a hillbilly, a country bumpkin, or an uncultured boy, but for me I accept the title with a sense of pride. It seems to me Jesus never resisted the title "Jesus of Nazareth." Before and after his death, it was a title connected to his life and ministry. Granted, it was a common method of that day to identify people (no last names so you were known by your name and your town such as Joseph of Arimathaea John 20:38). As we have discovered, Nazareth was not seen as a place to be proud of being from (John 1:46). Each and every time we see Jesus of Nazareth, we need to hear Jesus the Nazarene.

Despite the fact that Jesus was born in Bethlehem, he was known mostly for being from Nazareth. (Interestingly, I was born in Caribou, but have for all my life been associated with Perham, the town I was raised in.) There seems to have been some confusion over the fact even later in his ministry (John 7:42) when Jesus' enemies debated over the fact if He were the Messiah, He should have been born in Bethlehem. We know he was, but that fact seemingly wasn't common knowledge. To those who sought to kill him, he was Jesus the Nazarene. Jesus was seen as "the man from the other side of the track" or "the wrong side of town." At that time Nazareth had

A NAZARENE IN NAZARETH

become a deposit of many races, a mixed population with a rough dialect. Remember when Peter was recognized in a crowd because of his speech (Matthew 26:73)? Isn't it interesting that the very people that spotted Peter by his accent identified "this fellow was also with Jesus of Nazareth." (Matthew 26:71)

It has also become clear to me that Jesus honored his hometown by taking it as part of his name. He was not Jesus of Jerusalem, or Athens, or even Rome. So it is that the small, unknown town that became his earthly home has now become a town honor, not of disgrace, because he lived there. It has always been my desire to bring honor to my home town. I will forever be blessed if through my life and activities, I do not bring shame on the town that raised me. I hope that after my life is through, people who know of me will say that something good did come out of Perham, and his name was Barry.

THE NAZARENES OF NAZARETH

ACTS 24:5 . . . A ringleader of the sect of the Nazarenes.

Not only was the Christ known as Jesus of Nazareth, it wasn't long before His followers were also known as being from his hometown even though we can't verify that any of His disciples came from there.

As I have researched every verse and reference to Jesus' connection to Nazareth, the only individuals that seem to fit the sect of the Nazarenes is his mother and brothers (Act 1:14). Not until after Jesus death and resurrection does it appear that some of his brothers became believers. We know only of James and Jude (Judas) (Matthew 13:55) for sure because of their authorship of the books of James and Jude. It has become my belief however that all the brothers and the sisters (Matthew 13:56) did accept their older brother as the Christ. But why did men like Paul (a native of Tarsus Acts 22:3) become known as a Nazarene?

Many terms and titles were given to the early followers of Jesus, names like **"the way"** (Acts 9:2) and **"Christian"** (Acts 1:26), but for me the most inspiring has to be **"Nazarene."** We often forget that the names the enemies of Christ gave to His followers were not flattering names or complimentary names, but names to be despised and scorned. Granted, the name Christian has become an honored name over time, but at first it was a hated name. So too can we trace the use of the term Nazarenes. We have often used the original concept attached to that name such as when Nathanael asked Philip, *"Can there any good thing come out of Nazareth?"* (John 1:46) The only product of Nazareth is a Nazarene. Jesus was the most famous Nazarene to come out of Nazareth, but His was a future fame, not a readily accepted fame because he was eventually rejected and fell into reproach of the nation. His followers would have the same stigma connected to them for many years thereafter.

That is why when Paul was under arrest and brought before the Roman governor, he was called *"a pestilent fellow," "a mover of sedition," and "a ringleader of the sect of the Nazarenes"* (Acts 24:5). It was part of the derision placed on the followers of Christ by their enemies, and it was part of the burden the early believers had to bear in order to follow Jesus. Paul would later write, **"That I may know Him, and the power of His resurrection, and the fellowship of His sufferings, being made conformable unto His death."** (Philippians 3:10) Part of "the fellowship of His suffering" was in taking His name and any term associated with His name like Nazarene.

Part of our being identified with Christ is in the names people call us. What our enemies don't realize is that even in the names they call us they are connecting us with the One we love and adore. It is no great burden for us to be called His names, even to be called a Nazarene.

THE HONEY OF NAZARETH

Isaiah 7:15 Butter and honey shall He eat . . .

Another of the foods in the times of Jesus of Nazareth was honey, or at least this is the prophetic statement of Isaiah. I can't find a parallel verse in the gospels verifying this, but Jesus' cousin, John the Baptist, ate honey (Matthew 3:4) so why not Jesus? Once again I have something I can relate to my childhood upbringing and the life of Jesus in Nazareth.

Last autumn I was given a chance at 66 to relive a boyhood experience. Few of us get a chance to go back in time and relive a memorable event from our past. There is a family in my current church who raise bees. The Brennen's are country folks, and Mike's roots are in Aroostook County where my Perham is located. A few years ago Mike decided he wanted to follow his father's example and raise a few bees for honey. It was my joy when I was asked if I might like to help him gather the fall harvest. Why was I so excited?

When I became a teenager, my father decided that he would like to take on as a hobby the raising of bees. Dad had been inspired by our pastor. He bought three hives, and for that first summer we cared for these hives in a joint effort to produce some pure bee's honey. Our labors were rewarded late in September with a load of sweet honey. Nearly fifty years later I was walking with Mike Brennen to his three hives to do the same thing. With our bee nets over our heads and the smoker in my hand, we opened the top sections and began to remove the bees and take the honey comb. I was only stung once, and the pain was compensated one hundred fold by the jar of pure honey I received for my labor that day.

As I thought about my times in Perham with Dad's bees and the reliving of the experience with Mike's bees, I was struck with the thought that Jesus must have also witnessed and shared in the wonderful reward that

THE HONEY OF NAZARETH

comes from a summer's work of a group of bees. I know that the methods and means of collecting bee's honey were different in Jesus' day, but the end result was the same. I discovered that 61 times honey or the honey comb is mentioned in the Bible. It was a coveted product and much used in Bible times. Bees were known to deposit their sweet nectar in the crevices of rocks (Psalms 81:16) and in the hollows of trees. The Bible writers used honey as symbolic (Song of Solomon 4:11) of many things including the Word of God itself (Psalms 19:10). As Jesus tasted the honey from "a land flowing with milk and honey" (Exodus 3:17), He too must have enjoyed His creation's greatest sweetness.

I still enjoy the taste of pure bee's honey on toast and other breads, but what I enjoy most is another direct link between my experiences and the events in the life of my Lord and Saviour in Nazareth. Perham was not Nazareth and Nazareth was not Perham except when two boys were eating honey.

WORKSHOP IN NAZARETH

ACTS 10:38 How GOD anointed Jesus of Nazareth . . .

I was reading a devotional by James S. Stewart the other day, and it reminded me of our workshop on the family farm. It also taught me a valuable lesson. "**Jesus was the carpenter of Nazareth. It is impossible to exhaust the significance of the fact that for a great part of His life on earth the Son of God toiled with his hands, doing a joiner's work.** 'A workshop,' said Henry Drummond 'is not a place for making engines so much as a place for making men.' A workshop helped to make the soul of Christ. The devoted skill and labor that went into those Nazareth yokes and ploughs and cottage tables were rendered as an offering to God. Even then Jesus was 'about His Father's business.' Hence toil has been hallowed forever. The distinction between secular and sacred avocations vanishes. Hard work—whether manual labor or duty of business—is sacred when it is done as under the eyes of God. Very dear the cross of shame, where He took the sinner's blame, but he walked the same high road, and He bore the self-same load, when the carpenter of Nazareth made common things for God."

As I pondered those thoughts, my mind raced back to a time when I spent time in the workshop of the Blackstone homestead. Our workshop, machine shop, and repair shop was an old building in the woods just north of the main homestead buildings. During my years on the farm the building was surrounded by woods with an exit at both ends of the structure. The front entrance opened up to a shady lane that led to the Blackstone Road, while the back exit led to an open field behind the main cow barn. I can still see the times I drove tractors with broken farming equipment into that workshop so that Uncle Clayton could fix them. My father's cousin was the master mechanic of the farm. We rarely sent machinery away to be fixed.

WORKSHOP IN NAZARETH

Most repairs were corrected in the workshop, and most needed materials were made in the workshop. I wasn't much of a carpenter or a mechanic, but I see now I wasn't there for such things.

I suspect that Jesus was a good carpenter and his time in his father's workshop was profitable, not only in building things, but in developing the characteristics that would eventually be revealed in his earthly ministry. I too have been able after nearly five decades to understand the impact the family workshop has had on my spiritual ministry. I have been a pastor of four small churches in 45 years. The effect of my time in the workshop taught me the importance of allowing the skilled individuals of the church to do their job. As my father taught me quite early, ***"It isn't what you know, but who you know that knows."*** I learned early in both the workshop of the farm and the workshop of the church that some tasks are best left to others. Truly, Jesus left some works for us to do when He returned to His Father.

COUNSELOR OF NAZARETH

ISAIAH 9:6 . . . AND His name shall be called . . . counselor . . .

    As I looked and searched through the Bible for the best verses on peace, I also looked and searched through my collection of devotional writers to see what they wrote about **"the peace of God"** and **"the God of peace."** One of the great joys I have experienced in over sixty years of being a Christian are the men and women authors I have had the privilege to read. I see now they have become my *"counselors of peace"* (Proverbs 12:20). What joy and what peace have come to me as I have read of their experiences and their thoughts. I can say honestly that they have gotten me through many a tribulation time in my life. It is for this reason that hardly a day passes that I don't take some time to read and reread the devotionals they have written. A case in point is an article by Oswald Chambers. "Jesus said, 'Ye shall have tribulation' (John 16:33): not difficulties, but tribulation. But 'tribulation worketh patience' (Romans 5:3). Millstones are used to grind the corn to powder, and typify the sacredness of the discipline of life. 'No man shall take the nether or upper millstone to pledge; for he taketh a man's life to pledge.' (Deuteronomy 24:6) You have been having a snug time in the granary; then God brings you out and puts you under the millstone, and the first thing that happens is the grinding separation of which our Lord spoke: 'Blessed are ye when men shall . . . cast out your name as evil for the Son of Man's sake.' (Luke 6:22) Crushed for ever is any resemblance to the other crowd. Hands off! When God is putting His saint through the experience of the millstones. We are apt to want to interfere in the discipline of another saint. Do not hinder the production of the bread that is to feed the world! In the East the women sing as they grind the corn between the millstones. 'The sound of the millstones is music in the ears of God.' (Jeremiah 25:10) It is not music to the worlding, but the saint understands that His Father has a purpose in it all. Ill-tempered persons, hard circumstances, poverty, willful misunderstandings and estrangements are all millstones. Had Jesus any of these things in His life? Had He Not! He had a devil in His company for three years! He was continually thwarted and misunderstood by the Pharisees. And is the disciple above His Master? When these experiences come, remember that God has His eye on every detail. But beware! Lest the tiniest element of self-pity keeps God from putting us anywhere near the millstones!" Is there any wonder Jesus told us to "be of good cheer" at such times? Did He not also promise us His peace even under "the millstones" of life?

We know from our key verse printed above that Jesus of Nazareth would be known as "Counselor" and if you put that name with "Prince of Peace," He too was a *"counselor of peace,"* and I believe He started that ministry in Nazareth.

A SOWING SERMON FROM NAZARETH

LUKE 24:19 ... CONCERNING Jesus of Nazareth ...

Who of us doesn't know of the rewards of sowing seed? First, there is the reality that what you sow that shall you also reap (Galatians 6:7, 8). There is a divine order upon earth. There are certain precepts that are always true. Time and man can't change these divine precepts. One such truth is that if you sow a potato seed, you will reap potatoes. If you sow a corn seed, you will get corn. I saw this demonstrated time and time again on the family farm in Perham, Maine. It is impossible to trick God because it is His immutable law, both naturally and spiritually. T. Dewitt Talmadge once told this story. **"'How have you made out to live so long and be so well?' asked a young man of one who was ninety years of age. The old man took the younger to an orchard. Pointing to some large trees full of apples, he said, 'I planted those trees when I was a boy, and do you wonder that now I am permitted to gather the fruit of them?' 'Whatsoever a man soweth that shall he also reap.' We gather in old age what we plant in youth. Plant in early life the right kind of Christian character, and you will eat the luscious fruit in old age and gather the harvest in eternity. Why stay we on earth unless it be to grow?'"**

Not only is there the precept of "kind for kind," but there is also the concept of "the harvest is always larger than the sowing" (II Corinthians 9:10). I have watched my grandfather and my father sows a barrel of potatoes on a piece of land and gets back scores of barrels in return. Hannah sowed one child back to the Lord and got five in return (I Samuel 2:21). The little lad gave the Lord his lunch and in return enough food was distributed

A SOWING SERMON FROM NAZARETH

to feed thousands. I never saw a single potato reproduce in the potato bin, but once planted in the field, wow!

After **"ye reap what you sow"** and **"the harvest is always larger than the sowing,"** we come to the most difficult principle of all—***"the seed must die in order to live"*** (John 12:24) taught by Jesus Himself. I have on occasion dug up a potato seed after it was planted. The hardness of the potato had changed to the point it was soft to the touch. In the death of the potato comes the rebirth of a new potato plant that will, as we have seen, reproduce many times more than the original seed. I watched these simple precepts revealed on the potato farm that was the Blackstone homestead just as Jesus watched the precepts in the fields surrounding Nazareth. Over the years as a pastor, I have seen the spiritual application to that simple sowing in the hearts and lives of those I have had the privilege to pastor. What I have sown in them on Sunday, in time, I have seen flower and bloom in their character and conduct on Monday. Jesus too would later experience such a fulfillment of the sowing principles in the people of Galilee.

TWILIGHT IN NAZARETH

EZEKIEL 12:7 . . . I brought it forth in the twilight . . .

Many, many, many years ago someone wrote a song called "Just a Song at Twilight." The only reason I even know of this song, because I dare say I have never heard it sung and I know not of its message or melody, is the rereading of an old book given to me by my father in which the title was mentioned. I am thinking and praying for my father this morning as I type away at my old Apple (1988) computer. Dad is in the hospital. Dad has been a very healthy man most of his life, but the last few years (he's 84) have been rough. Today as I read again Vance Havner's (Dad's favorite author) article on "Just a Song at Twilight" I was brought to the reality that my dad is at the twilight of his life. (Yet in God's providence Dad would live nearly a decade more!) I believe Jesus experienced such a time in his earthly father's life as well.

I still recall the twilights of my youth when for just a few minutes the family would watch the sunset. We never took notice that another day in our peaceful life was dying. Mine was a Norman Rockwell kind of childhood. Do you remember that amazing artistry that once covered the front cover of the Saturday Evening Post? (I believe my parents still have a few copies of that magazine in the attic of their farm house.) How those simple, but telling, pictures of Americana still pull at the heartstrings of our aging hearts and still stir us to wonderful recollections of our past. Such is the stirring in my heart this fallish morning on the coast of Maine as I am struck with the reality that my dad has reached twilight, and he needs a song.

Nostalgia, however, will not change the sad feeling that came to my heart last night when Mother called to tell me of Dad's latest struggle. I hurt for the man I call father because he doesn't know how to be sick. We talked just a few weeks ago at a family reunion of how he felt in these twilight years. His thoughts were of finishing his course, of keeping his faith, (II Timothy 4:6) and the time of his departure being at hand, but what if it isn't? Sometimes twilight lasts awhile. On those evenings when the sky is clear and the sun hangs low on the horizon without interference from clouds or storms, twilight lingers long. I don't know how my father will face the difficult times just before his sun sets, but as Vance wrote to end his article, so I pray this morning for my dad at twilight. **"I am still trying to find 'Just a Song at Twilight'. It is twilight with me and with this age. Just any song will not do for such twilight."**

I have enjoyed most of the twilights of my life, but I am afraid that the one coming in my father's life will not be a memorable one (and it wasn't, the last 555 days of his life were terrible for him and his family as he struggled in a Veteran's Home and a failing mind). I will go through it with him and the rest of my family. I only wish I could find that song. For I know well my twilight is coming and I too will need that song, a song Jesus never needed for his twilight would come at a young age!

SCRAPING IN NAZARETH

EZEKIEL 26:4 . . . I will also scrape . . .

I have come to the belief that there is **"a science of scraping."** This reality struck me just yesterday as I watched my wife prepare a potato scallop for a supper on the shore. We have some church friends from Pennsylvania that vacation each summer on Contention Cove in Surry, Maine, and attend our church. They soon will be heading back home so we decided to take them supper and enjoy the million-dollar view from their porch one last time. As my wife asked me to scrape the peelings off the new potatoes we had brought back from Aroostook County following a family reunion, I was taken back in time when we scraped our way through the fall season, as no doubt Jesus did in Nazareth.

Did you ever scrape a fresh picked apple or a newly dug potato? I think we all know about peeling an apple or a potato, but scraping might be a new technique to some. When an apple or a potato is fresh, the skins are fragile. Most wait until the skins are tougher before picking because this helps in preventing damage. A bruised apple or potato is hard to sell, but I am not talking about selling. I am recalling the times we eat our fruit right off the tree or right out of the ground. This strategy is used when you don't like the peelings of either the apple or the potato. Could I confess something to you now? When my wife asked me to help her peel the potatoes the other night, I was for just cleaning them and not bothering with the peelings. I must admit that when I make French fries, I don't peel the potatoes. When I eat an apple, I don't peel the apple. I am a skin man, Courtland's or cobblers.

I know there are some reading these memories that agree with me, but could I confess something else to you? I am also lazy when it comes to apples and potatoes. I am in too much of a hurry to waste my time scraping and peeling my fruit or vegetable. Yes, I eat my carrots raw, and any

SCRAPING IN NAZARETH

vegetable I like I would rather have it uncooked. Lazy! Cooking takes time, peeling takes time, scraping takes time. In this harried and hurried age we don't have time to scrape or rub the potato in our hands until it is shining white or until the apple reveals it's white center. Scraping has gone the way of whittling. Scraping a potato is symbolic of a simpler time, an unhurried time when we took time, had time to enjoy the natural pleasures of an autumn day, a time when we had time to listen to the final concert of the songbirds of summer, at time when we had time to watch the sunset and the sunrise, a time when we could take the time to stroll along the shore and watch the windjammers settle into Contention Cove in advance of a sea storm.

Sometimes my dear wife has to slow me down by asking me to peel the potatoes and to scrape the squash. Jesus was in no hurry to leave Nazareth either. It took him thirty years.

A TOURIST IN NAZARETH

MATTHEW 4:13 AND LEAVING Nazareth, He came and dwelt in . . .

If I live on the coast of Maine until next spring (we are just a few days away from the start of autumn), I will have lived as long in Ellsworth as I did in my hometown of Perham. I am shocked by this reality, but the truth of this came home to me just a few weeks ago when I returned to my boyhood home for a family reunion and felt like a tourist.

As I travelled around the familiar areas of Aroostook County, I sensed for the first time that I was a stranger in a foreign land. Granted, the names of the towns were the same and many of the houses and buildings were the same, but something was different. I even visited people I had known my entire life, like Lily Harris, my old Children's Church teacher. Lily has been a resident of the Presque Isle Nursing Home for nearly a decade now. I visit her each and every time I am in the County, but 93 years has changed my once vibrant teacher. What I saw in her I relived at the home of my Uncle Clayton and in the life of my father and mother. News of the failing health of other aunts and uncles caused me to see the people of my youth differently. Family was becoming strangers and old neighbors were becoming foreigners.

If the people were changing, so were the places of my boyhood. As I travelled from Cross Lake (my sister and brother-in-law have a new camp on its shores) to Houlton, I looked again at the places that were once a part of my life. Washburn wasn't the small town it uses to be. Perham, my hometown, lacked the farming it once had. The town of Westfield where I pastored for eight year was just another passing-through place to somewhere else. At times I thought to myself, "Did I really live here?" Oh, memories came back of experiences and events, but twenty-two years have changed those vivid memories into shadows and flashbacks to another time and age that seem a fantasy rather than a fact. Did Jesus feel that way about Nazareth, too?

There was a time when I thought I would return to the county of my birth. At least twice since I left Aroostook, I have tried to get back or go back, but each time the door closed. Now it seems I will never go back despite the fact I have roots and property (a home building that I sold in 2017) waiting for me there, but will I? The longer I stay away the more it seems that home is not there, but here (the coast of Maine). I am not saying I won't go back. I know I will because there will always be happenings that will draw me back, but I have come to grips with the reality that I will always go back as a tourist, a tourist that will revisit the past, the people, and the places that shaped my life and sent me away. I believe I am cured from the desire to return there to live. A tourist and a stranger in my own land is something that I thought would never happen to me. Jesus said of his hometown, "A prophet is without honor in his own country." (Matthew 13:57)

A PRAYER FROM NAZARETH

MATTHEW 6:9 AFTER THIS manner therefore pray ye . . .

Do you remember being taught to pray? Do you remember the first prayer you prayed? Do you remember the words of that prayer? Recently, I finished W. Phillip Keller's book on "A Layman Looks at the Lord's Prayer." As I read this wonderful observation on the world's most famous prayer, I was also working on my book "Another Day in Nazareth." I got to thinking, "Who prayed the Lord's Prayer first? Was it the Lord Himself? Was the pattern for all prayers developed during Jesus' years as a boy in Nazareth?"

I was taught to pray by my mother in those final moments of the day in Perham. I still recall that kneeling-beside-my-bedside prayer, "Now I lay me down to sleep. I pray the Lord my soul to keep. If I should die before I wake, I pray the Lord my soul to take." And it was also my mother that first taught me the words to Jesus' memorable prayer. Long before I could read, I had placed in my mind the words of the Lord's Prayer. Long before I understood one word, the words became a part of my memory. To this day I can repeat these famous words without even thinking. Now I ponder, not the first time or the thousands of times I have prayed this prayer, but the first time it was formulated in the mind of Christ in Nazareth.

Why did Jesus pick these simple sixty-six words to express his prayer to His Father? Repeated over and over again for twenty centuries now, it was the first utterance that spoke volumes to the heart of God. The Son's deepest emotion to what he thought and what he asked and how he honored his Father. Remember, he was human now, yet inside he was divine. **"For in Him dwelleth all the fullness of the Godhead bodily."** (Colossians 2:9) This was in reality a prayer to Himself, and yet despite the billions of times this prayer has been prayed by the millions of people that have prayed it, it has never and will never lose one ounce of effectiveness. Repetition, familiarity, or time can't change this perfect prayer. I love the way Phillip Keller put it. **"The profound, eternal concepts compressed into its few, concise phrases shine with enduring brilliance. These truths radiated from the very heart of our Lord and He moved among men. They embrace the deepest secrets of God, quietly stated in human language of disarming simplicity. Some of the petitions included in this prayer by Christ were utterly revolutionary. If fully grasped by us, they can overturn much of our own wrong thinking about God."**

So was it by his bedside that Jesus first prayed these words? Was his mother there when he uttered this famous supplication for the first time? Or was it in the secret of his mind that he first formed this petition that he would teach his disciples years later? I don't know the answer to these questions, but I do know I learned it in my Nazareth.

A PETITION FROM NAZARETH

MATTHEW 6:9 OUR FATHER which art in Heaven . . .

Can't you hear Jesus now? When He taught His disciples how to pray, He picked, I believe, a petition He had been praying for years, thirty years in Nazareth as He waited His time. In Nazareth this classic petition would have begun, "My Father which art in Heaven . . ."

One of the blessings of my childhood was a father. So many children today grow up not knowing their father or being abused by their father. I never knew a minute of my boyhood that my father wasn't there. Dad worked away from my home, but he was never more than a few miles away. Being raised on a working potato and dairy farm had its advantages in the category of a father/son relationship. I was either working with dad or very close to dad no matter the day, month, or year. Jesus did have an earthly father, but, as we have already mentioned, for how long we don't know. Joseph was much older than Mary, and Joseph seems to be gone by the time Jesus is grown. We know Jesus was around Joseph at least until he was twelve (Luke 2:42), but even in that famous trip to Jerusalem we see Jesus was more focused on his heavenly Father. "How is it that ye sought me? Wist ye not that I must be about my Father's business?" (Luke 2:49)

So it doesn't surprise me that Jesus used this title of "Father" in his prayer. It was a Father/Son relationship that would mark the connection of the Godhead throughout Jesus' earthly ministry. Even towards the end of his earthly ministry Jesus would tell his disciples, "I and my Father are one." (John 10:30) It is not a stretch for me to say that as a boy in Nazareth Jesus began his prayers, "My Father which art in heaven." I do believe Jesus saw fairness, honesty, decency in Joseph, but it was to his Father that he directed his prayers and petitions. We know he prayed much as an adult so why do we not also conclude that he prayed much as a child, and of course there was that focus on "heaven."

Nazareth was Jesus' earthly dwelling, but heaven was always home and the One that lived there. Oh, God is here wherever here is, but He is there also. I believe the only time that the Godhead was separated was at Calvary, but Jesus had separated himself from the abode of heaven to be our Savior, and though they were one in the Spirit, there was a great gap between Nazareth and heaven in the reality of human versus divine. Have we ever pondered just how much Jesus had to sacrifice to become the boy of Nazareth? Have we ever thought through what a condescension it was for the Son of God to take on "the form of a servant" (Philippians 2:7) of Nazareth? Have we ever meditated on just how difficult it was for God to become man? It is now no wonder to me that Jesus got great satisfaction out of talking to his Father, and so he prayed, "My Father which art . . . ."

RESPECT FROM NAZARETH

MATTHEW 6:9 ... HALLOWED be thy name.

I have never known a time I was not instructed, challenged, and desired to honor the name of God. Being raised in a Christian family, I was taught to pray in the name of Jesus, sing to the honor of that name, and use it only when the situation and circumstances warranted its use. The Perham of my boyhood was a place where the respect and reverence for the name of God was honored. Granted, there were times when I heard the name of God used in vain and abused by the few, and it shocked me then as it disturbs me now. I believe that these concepts were also practiced in Nazareth because "Thy Name" highlights and underlines in every aspect the very Person of God Himself.

How did Jesus feel as he walked the streets and byways of Nazareth and heard His Father's name used in vain? Was it the reason he put as the first petition in his pattern prayer this precept that would honor the character of God, the reputation of God, the identity of God, and the very person of God Himself? I do believe that there were people in Perham who were ignorant of the eternal, enduring, everlasting nature of the Almighty just as there were people in Nazareth with the same ignorance. Respect for God is more often than not a taught respect, but I have discovered that in every human being there is a piece of the soul that demands our reverence to a higher being even if we haven't as yet been taught who that higher being is. It is the conscience of man that first creates the belief that I had better respect God because of Who He is.

"Hallowed" has become the key word to the understanding of this aspect of the Lord's Prayer because of the King James Version of the Bible, but unfortunately "hallow" is not used much anymore and it has become just another word we use without seeking its meaning. The concept I believe

Jesus was trying to convey was that His Father's name was to be kept holy. God is holy, and His name is holy. "Holy" derives its roots from the old Anglo-Saxon words of *halig* and *hale*. These words denote the precept of being set apart or something that is very special, pure, and whole. Again, I like Keller's amplification of Hallowed Be Thy Name, **"May you be honored, revered, and respected because of Who you are. May your reputation, name, person, and character be kept untarnished, uncontaminated, unsullied. May nothing be done to debase or defame your record?"**

Jesus taught in Nazareth as I was taught in Perham that the name of God was not to be scorned and that no sarcasm was to be cast against it. Despite the sneering and the cursing that is now associated with the Holy Name, I for one still stand in awe that we are even able to use it, but we are if we use it to honor Him who was given "a name which is above every name." (Philippians 2:9)

THE KINGDOM STARTED IN NAZARETH

MATTHEW 6:10 THY KINGDOM come...

Every event, organization, or life has to start somewhere. For me, it was the sleepy, valley hamlet of Perham. I was raised on a small, county farm in northern Maine, and it was upon that foundation I built the life and work that is me today. When Jesus Christ finally settled in Nazareth after years on the road (Bethlehem, Jerusalem, Bethlehem, and Egypt), the "kingdom" began. In Jesus' classic parable on the pounds (Luke 19:11–27), He tells of a nobleman who travels to a far country to receive a kingdom. I have come to understand that the nobleman is Christ and the kingdom is the millennium kingdom. If as we suspect, Jesus began formulating the Lord's Prayer in Nazareth, then the phrase "thy Kingdom come" is in reference to the millennium kingdom that Jesus Himself will establish when He returns again to earth.

Jesus told his disciples about the pounds because they thought that he was heading to Jerusalem to establish the kingdom at that time (Luke 19:11) when in reality he was heading to a criminal's crucifixion at Calvary. Even after Jesus' death, burial, and resurrection, his followers still thought he would start his kingdom then (Act 1:6). Once again, Jesus had to inform the disciples that he first had to go away (like the nobleman that went to a far country to receive a kingdom), and only upon his return would the kingdom be established. Established then, but started in Nazareth is how I see it because Jesus' kingdom started within the hearts of man (Luke 17:20, 21), and the first heart to know this truth was Jesus himself. Until Jesus is established on the throne of one's heart, until he is the king of the kingdom of one's life, there will be no loyalty to the King of the millennium kingdom.

THE KINGDOM STARTED IN NAZARETH

I was living in Perham when I sincerely and earnestly and genuinely allowed Jesus to come into my life and establish His kingdom in my life (I Corinthians 3:16). The kingdom of Christ is being formed to this day in the heart of lives of those who have made Him "King of their lives." As Jesus lived his early life out in Nazareth, little did the citizens of Nazareth realize that "The King" was already in their midst. The most important ingredient for any kingdom is a king; without a king there can be no kingdom. This is why I believe we have before us another wonderful example of the importance of "another day in Nazareth" in the life of Jesus. He was starting his kingship undercover, to live and work among us, to know of us and about us, to know best how to serve us as any good king would do. Jesus is no monarch that cares little for his subjects, who is not willing to bear the burdens of the citizens of his country. Nazareth showed just how far our King was willing to humble Himself to serve us.

THE WILL OF NAZARETH

MATTHEW 6:10 THY WILL be done in earth, as it is in heaven.

When Jesus came to earth, He came to do the Father's will (John 6:38), and part of that "will" was Nazareth.

The central theme of this book, "Another Day in Nazareth," has been to highlight and underline the blessings we sometimes miss when we fail to realize that even the 'Nazareth" of our lives was established squarely in the Father's will. We have focused our attention in the life of Christ during his development years in Nazareth as a way to see the reason for my years in Perham or your years in the "Perham" of your life. As I near the end of this writing project, I am closing in on the end of a second eighteen-year experience in Nazareth. I lived eighteen years in Perham in my youth, and in just a few short months I will have lived eighteen years in Ellsworth. In the last few years I have wanted to move on, do something different, in a different place, yet I have been led by the Lord to stay put, to stay in my second Nazareth. Why? That God's will on earth for me would be the same as God's willed for me in heaven.

God's will, both earthly and heavenly, is the simple intent and intention of God's desire for His people. Jesus came to earth to show his followers that like Him they too must yield to the Father's will. It is impossible to sever the will of God from God Himself yet He has given us free-will to either yield to His will or do our own will. This piece of the Lord's Prayer is for the intent that we accept God's heavenly will on earth, and Jesus' life in Nazareth is the proof that we can do just that. God's will is based on what He thinks is best for us. Despite our question of why thirty years in an isolated Galilee town Jesus accepted the Father's will, (and I am convinced because He could do that) He would and did accept the Father's will about Calvary

THE WILL OF NAZARETH

(Matthew 26:39). Our Nazareth has to do more with our learning how to yield to the Father's will then it has to do with simply living in Nazareth.

The ultimate will of God finds its best reality in the odd and strange requests and directions of God. Think with me for awhile of the unusual places God places His servants: Joseph in Egypt, Moses in Sinai, David in the backwater places of Canaan just one step away from King Saul, and what of Daniel and his friends? Yet it was in these places these mighty men of God learned the secret of complete cooperation between their will and God's will. It was in the town of Perham that I too learned this secret, and I can honestly say it has been that wisdom that has allowed me to yield to the Lord's will each and every time He has changed my life. It is the reason I was able to go to Eastport and Ellsworth even though I wanted to go to other places and parishes. Yet, as I look back on these places now, I see, as Jesus saw, that Nazareth was the best place for me at the time.

DAILY BREAD IN NAZARETH

MATTHEW 6:11 GIVE US this day our daily bread.

    Of all the phrases of the Lord's Prayer, it is this piece of Jesus' pattern prayer I remember best. Every day, three times a day I heard my father give grace at the family meal. Those were the days when families ate together. Ours was a daily pattern of breakfast, lunch, and supper (I didn't know of "dinner" until I left the county). These meals and Dad's prayer was only changed if my brothers, sisters, and I were in school, and then only for lunch. If we ate out, it was only to our grandparent's homes, but a prayer was offered there as well. Our daily bread came from the farm because rarely did Mother go to a market, and if she did it was only to buy those things we couldn't produce on the homestead. Ours was a truly rural existence, and I learned at a very early age that my parents and grandparents believed that God was the ultimate giver of our daily bread despite the long hours they worked in the fields.

    Can you imagine how Jesus must have felt when he went from a "no-need" place (heaven) to a daily-need place (Nazareth)? We know of Jesus emptying Himself of all but the Godhead (Colossians 2:9). The One that was never hungry got hungry. The One that was never thirsty got thirsty. The One that never got tired got tired. The One that never had to travel on foot, travelled on foot. The One that never had to think about his daily bread, thought and prayed for his daily bread. Jesus had limited himself to earthly limitations, and, as we all know, the greatest of these is daily bread. The One that had cursed man that through the sweat of his brow would he eat bread (Genesis 3:19) was now with the sweat of his brow earning His bread. I like the way Phillip Keller explained this concept. **"As the carpenter craftsman, working in Joseph's wood making shop in Nazareth, Jesus knew all about this. He later had to support His widowed mother**

DAILY BREAD IN NAZARETH

and young siblings by the strength of His muscles, skill of His hands, and sweat of His brow. Hacking and chopping, sawing and planning, shaping and fitting the tough, twisted olive wood and hard, heavy acacia timber that grew in Galilee was no child's play. It was back-breaking toil that turned trees into cattie yokes, plows, tables, and candlesticks that he could sell for a few shekels to buy bread." Truly, Jesus knew all too well of daily bread.

Jesus could have used his divine power (Matthew 28:18) to provide his daily bread, but there is no indication that until he began his earthly preaching, teaching, and healing ministry that he did. He was determined in his Nazareth to live like us, and in that I see him bowing his head and asking his Father for the strength and ability to meet the need of daily bread for his mother, his brothers, and his sisters (Mark 6:3). If he prayed such a prayer, doesn't it seem proper that we would pray such a prayer as well?

FORGIVENESS IN NAZARETH

MATTHEW 6:12 AND FORGIVE us our debts, as we forgive our debtors.

One doesn't live long on this planet without needing forgiveness from someone. I still remember those times on the farm in Perham when my mother would act as mediator between my sister and me. I don't remember a lot of fights or disagreements, but as with any sister and brother relationship Sylvia and I had our share of hurt feelings, misunderstandings, and encounters that required one or both of us to forgive the other. Was it in Nazareth that Jesus first learned the earthly need of forgiveness? I know that he being God already had divine forgiveness in his heart, but the practical administration of forgiveness was in my opinion played out and practiced in Jesus' life in Nazareth.

When one looks at the various translations of the verse printed above, you come up with some amazing ideas:

"Forgive us our trespasses" (Knox).
"Forgive us our shortcomings" (Weymouth).
"Forgive us what we owe to you" (Phillips).
"Forgive us our sins" (Living Bible).
"Forgive us our resentments" (Amplified).
"Forgive us the wrong we have done" (New English).
"Forgive us our debts" (King James).

This I know. Jesus committed no trespasses, had no shortcomings, owed nobody anything, had no resentments, did no wrongs, accumulated no debts because he committed no sins (II Corinthians 5:21); therefore, He never had to ask anybody for forgiveness, but how often did he have to forgive?

FORGIVENESS IN NAZARETH

As with the other lessons we have learned about Jesus in this series of articles on the phrases of The Lord's Prayer in relationship to Jesus' days in Nazareth, I believe the reason he was so quick to forgive the soldiers at the foot of the cross (Luke 23:34) was that he had so often done it in Nazareth. From living with the "perfect" in heaven, Jesus was now living with debtors, trespassers, sinners, and offenders—everyone. There was not one individual, family, friend, neighbor, customer, or stranger that didn't or won't do Him some wrong. Was He cheated? Was He yelled at? Was He robbed? Was He offended? Was He spoken ill of? Was He sworn at? Who knows in the nearly thirty years in Nazareth how often the people he lived with committed some kind of sin against him, yet this we know. He forgave each and every offense. It was the Apostle Paul who would write to the Ephesians this classic illustration on forgiveness: ***"And be ye kind one to another, tenderhearted, forgiving one another, even as God for Christ's sake hath forgiven you."*** (Ephesians 4:32) Jesus set the standard high!

TEMPTATION IN NAZARETH

MATHEW 6:13 AND LEAD us not into temptation . . .

Jesus never sinned, but he was tempted. "For we have not an high priest which cannot be touched with the feeling of our infirmities; but was in all points tempted like as we are, yet without sin" (Hebrews 4:15). There seems to be this popular misconception that Jesus never faced temptation until he was led out into the wilderness by the Spirit to be tempted by Satan (Matthew 4:1). If he was tempted as we are tempted, then he must have been tempted in Nazareth.

Do you remember your first temptation? Was it a temptation to swear about something? Was it a temptation to steal something? Was it a temptation to lie about something? Each of us has plenty to remember about our childhood in relationship to temptation, as Jesus did. The difference between him and me is that he never yielded to temptation, but I often did. They say confession is good for the soul so let me share a boyhood temptation and the time I yielded to the old nature and sinned.

Perhaps, the greatest failing in my childhood was the lies I told my third and fourth grade teacher (I only had one). I didn't like school so to get through I would lie about finishing my homework, reading my assignments, and completing my tests. Because I had a hard time learning to read, I was always behind. I did have a sharp enough mind to figure how I could get around my teacher, especially when I had an older teacher that was getting a bit forgetful herself. My lies and deception worked well enough so that I thought I was getting away with it, and I did for years. However, I eventually got a teacher that saw through my game, and I was caught. I had wasted a number of years of valuable education because of my yielding to temptation. Thankfully, that teacher who finally saw through my lies was willing in my sixth year to work with me until I was able to make up for

TEMPTATION IN NAZARETH

some of the lost time. I still suffer to this day with a weakness in reading, spelling, and grammar.

Jesus, however, knew the meaning of this very important, but rarely sung, hymn. **"Yield not to temptation, for yielding is sin; each victory will help you some other to win; fight manfully onward, dark passions subdue; look ever to Jesus, He'll carry you through. Shun evil companions, bad language distain; God's name hold in reverence, nor take it in vain; be thoughtful and earnest, kind-hearted and true; look ever to Jesus, He'll carry you through. To him that overcometh, God giveth a crown; through faith we will conquer, though often cast down; He who is our Savior, our strength will renew; look ever to Jesus, He'll carry you through. Ask the Savior to help you, comfort, strengthen, and keep you; He is willing to aid you, He will carry you through."**

Such truth took Jesus through his life in Nazareth sinless. Oh, that I had allowed Him to carry me through in Perham.

DELIVERANCE FROM NAZARETH

MATTHEW 6:13 ... BUT deliver us form evil; for thine is the kingdom, and the power, and the glory, forever. Amen.

Eventually, we all will be delivered from "Nazareth." Even Jesus would be delivered from his time there. I too was delivered from Perham in 1969. Like Jesus I have gotten a chance to return on occasions, but my time in my "Nazareth" seems to be over. I am still in my second "Nazareth" (Ellsworth), and I don't know when the good Lord will move me out. This project has opened my eyes to so many similarities between my Nazareth (Perham or Ellsworth) and Jesus' Nazareth that I have been blessed. What Jesus endured, I am enduring, and I know, like with him, my time is short.

Jesus was delivered from the evil that was this world and Nazareth. I too can be thankful that the Almighty has delivered me. I still remember when I was given the phrase that has sustained my praise all these years: "saved from" versus "saved out." So many have been saved out of loveless lives, horrible habits, and terrible transgressions. I was saved and delivered from so much. I sinned plenty, but I was delivered and didn't have to experience many a sin because of my 'Nazareth' days. Because of the godly examples and godly teaching of my parents, my pastor, and the godly people God placed me with, I can now reap the benefits of such a place called Perham. Satan, sin, and my own self-will was always present, and at times I yielded, but most of the time I resisted temptation. I believe it was because at an early age I was taught to pray "deliver me from evil."

Perham, as with Nazareth, was a trying, testing, and tempting time for me, but I can clearly see now that I was delivered from so much. While others have testimonies of being saved out of rebellion, disbelief, iniquities

DELIVERANCE FROM NAZARETH

of all kinds, I was delivered from such evils. It is for this reason I came at the age of seven to believe that His was the "kingdom" and the "power" and the "glory," and this is how it will be "forever." I celebrated my sixtieth spiritual birthday this spring. It was in Perham that I first heard His voice, believed His words, and started to follow His lead. I had a few detours, but not many. I learned well, I see now, in my 'Nazareth" to wait on Him, watch for Him, and work ultimately with Him. His glorious goodness has followed me (Psalms 23:6), His gigantic greatness has sustained me, and His generous graciousness has blessed me through 240 (60 times 4) seasons of my life.

The Lord's Prayer contains many a truth that must be understood before it is prayed, but the truth that has inspired me most is the reality that Jesus no doubt practiced these precepts of prayer while living an obscure life in Nazareth. This tells me that any one of us in our unknown "Nazareth" can do the same thing. If we ask for "deliverance," He has promised us deliverance.

POSTLUDE: JESUS OF NAZARETH

MARK 1:24 SAYING, LET us alone; what have we to do with Thee, thou Jesus of Nazareth?

We end as we began, why Jesus of Nazareth? Why thirty years of a thirty-three year spiritual mission spent in an out-of-the-way, small, no account town? Why would the eternal Godhead choose a village that had such a bad reputation? *"Can there any good thing come out of Nazareth?"* (John 1:46) What was Christ doing in Joseph's carpenter shop all those years? (Mark 6:3) What was he doing in Nazareth?

After months of pondering and sharing my own personal experiences from Perham and applying them to similar, possible events in Nazareth, it was finally these verses in Hebrews that gave me my first real clue into why Nazareth. "Who in the days [including days in Nazareth] of His flesh, when He had offered up prayers and supplications with strong crying and tears unto Him that was able to save Him from death, and was heard in that He feared; though He were a Son, yet LEARNED HE OBEDIENCE by the things which He suffered; and BEING MADE PERFECT, He became the author of eternal salvation unto all them that obey him." (Hebrews 5:7–9 *emphasis mine*) I have always been taught that Jesus knew everything, but Paul suggests that Jesus was in Nazareth to learn something. Now I understand better these two verses in Luke's account. *"And the child grew, and waxed strong in spirit, filled with wisdom: and the grace of God was upon Him . . . And Jesus increased in wisdom and stature and in favor with God and man."* (Luke 2:40, 52) Jesus was in Nazareth learning about earthly obedience, earthly wisdom, and earthly favor. Now I see the difference between a heavenly obedience and an earthly obedience. God the Son had

POSTLUDE: JESUS OF NAZARETH

yielded to the will of His Father, but could He humble himself and yield to the will of His mother and Joseph? Luke records this after Jesus' Jerusalem trip at twelve. **"And He went down with them, and came to Nazareth, and was subject unto them . . . "** (Luke 2:51)

Now I see why Nazareth. And now I see why Perham. If the Son of God must learn obedience, then so must I. If Jesus needed to be humbled, then so must I. Obedience, humility, and wisdom are learned virtues, and the only way to learn it is through practice. Jesus was practicing in Nazareth for His ministry in Galilee. I was practicing in Perham for my ministry in Ellsworth. I have said it for years, but a fuller understanding has only come through this "another day in Nazareth" study that Perham was my seminary; that I learned more practical lessons of the ministry on the farm then I ever did at college; and that one of my best professors was my father as I worked in his "carpenter's shop." Is it any wonder after thirty years of schooling that God the Father said, *"This is my beloved Son, in whom I am well pleased."* (Matthew 3:17)

I am learning from this lesson that I should not complain where my Father sends me. I should not quarrel about my environment. If God put Jesus into Nazareth and its day in and day out petty experiences, then He will do the same with me. Ultimately, I am being trained, molded, and transformed **"to be conformed to the image of His Son"** (Romans 8:29), and if that means a Nazareth in my life then that means I must, like Jesus, endure, increase, and grow in wisdom and favor in my Nazareth. That means I must survive the sordid saints in my life, the small tasks in my job, and the vexations of the "daily grind." I can't resent the trials that come in my Nazareth, and I can't be perplexed by the countless unanswered prayers to "please get me out of Nazareth." Is that what Paul was talking about when he said that "he offered up prayers and supplications with crying and tears?" I have only always thought of His time in Gethsemane in relationship to such weeping, but now I wonder if He did a lot of crying in Nazareth as well.

If you learn anything from my little trip back to Perham and Nazareth, my prayer is that you will learn as I have that Nazareth is God's appointed place of practice, of learning, of education in humility, patience, and obedience. Paul wrote to the believers in Philippi, "Not that I speak in respect of want: for I have learned, in whatsoever state [Nazareth] I am, therewith to be content. I know both how to be abased, and I know how to abound: everywhere [Perham] and in all things I am instructed both to be full and to be hungry, both to abound and to suffer need, I can do all things through

POSTLUDE: JESUS OF NAZARETH

Christ which strengtheneth me." (Philippians 4:11–13) It takes a Nazareth to learn this. Just about every virtue, though found in the Son of God before He came, was relearned through His Nazareth experiences. Paul would also write in Hebrews, "Seeing then we have a great high priest that is passed into the heavens, Jesus the Son of God, let us hold fast our profession. For we have not an high priest which cannot be touched with the feeling of our infirmities; but was in all points tempted like as we are, yet without sin." (Hebrews 4:14, 15) Jesus knew of my Perham experiences because of His Nazareth experiences.

It was Henry Drummond that said, **"Do not grudge the hand that is molding the still to shapeless image within you."** That image is Christ, and what we are becoming is what He became through His days in Nazareth. This is why we can relate to Him, and He to us. He knows of "another day in Nazareth," and His example (I Peter 2:21) is to help us learn what He learned, and be perfected as He was made perfect through His years in Nazareth. Take heart, my dear travelling companion in "another day in Nazareth," because you too are learning obedience and humility. Once you are finished you'll hear, "This is my beloved son in whom I am well pleased; well done, good and faithful servant." And it was in this that our Lord and Saviour Jesus Christ might have been the most faithful in his 'Nazareth Days'. I would like to close with this article that first appeared in the "Charlotte Observer" on June 8, 1930, exactly 88 years to the day I finished this book project. It was written by a 29 year old man by the name of Vance Havner under the title of "Life's Little Loyalties" and for me he summaries the message I have tried to get across in "Another Day in Nazareth" and I quote: **"It is a dull, ordinary day. I am clerking in a little country store. Farmers are in the fields. Once in a while a car drifts by. All the birds are quiet in the shade. Across the hot sky a vagabond cloud floats now and then. It is a sultry, monotonous, commonplace day. Nothing exciting or interesting, no thrilling happening, no brilliant thought, no fine feelings, no noble inspiration. I am lazy, trifling, stupid, and unambitious. Such days we all know. No life can stay on a high key all the time. No one runs all full steam, top pressure, day in and day out. Into every life comes the dull, drab seasons when nothing seems to kindle the pale embers of the spirit; nothing stirs the jaded soul. One reads and the same page that has enchanted us at other times is boresome. We try to think and the mind stalls. Perhaps we pray, and heaven seems locked. We can hardly endure ourselves. Others are tiresome and the whole world is**

POSTLUDE: JESUS OF NAZARETH

hateful. We feel toward everything like the scoffer toward music when he sneered: 'What are you crying about with your Wagner and your Brahms? It is only horsehair scraping on catgut!' Yet we have no days more important than these. They test us as no others do. Anyone can be fine and splendid and noble once in a while when some special occasion stretches them to highest tension. The commonest soul may strain up to a fair showing in some big moment. It is the pale, tedious, insipid day that reveals our real soul stuff for what we are (when we are not trying) is what we really are. It is said that no man is a hero to his valet. Few characters can carry through life's commonplace stretches without a breakdown somewhere. The temper will snap, the ideals will fade, and cynicism and unpleasantness mar the spirit. Great is the man who can stand by the stuff and play the game when every bit of inspiration seems drained and nothing seems to matter. Most of us can measure up to a big chance once in a while, but not so many are true to life's little loyalties, when the world does not notice and we do not seem to care. So instead of regarding such days as a loss, give them double attention. If you can master them, you never will face anything harder. If you can conquer the commonplace you need fear nothing. For they are the toughest stretches on this pilgrimage and more fade out along the ordinary grind than ever fall in the spectacular collapses. Indeed, here is where the chain of character is forged; here we build most of the structure of our souls. For great spirits are not made in dazzling exploits and hair-raising performances; they are slowly and tediously grown by sturdy devotion to the best in the old grind of day by day, the school of life's little loyalties. SOMETIMES I THINK JESUS SPENT THIRTY OF HIS THIRTY-THREE YEARS IN THE ORDINARY ROUTINE OF NAZARETH, CONQUERING THE COMMONPLACE. NOTHING EXCITING HAPPENED THERE, BUT ALL THE WHILE THE GREATEST ACHIEVEMENT OF HISTORY WAS BEING REALIZED: JESUS WAS WELDING TOGETHER THE GREATEST CHARACTER OF ALL TIME. AND HE DID IT BY STEADY DEVOTION TO THE ETERNAL AMONG LIFE'S LITTLE LOYALTIES. Your worst days may be your best days. And sometime what seemed biggest moments may, in the perspective of time, become your poorest!" Don't ignore 'another day in Nazareth'.

Barry Blackstone
June 8, 2018

www.ingramcontent.com/pod-product-compliance
Lightning Source LLC
Chambersburg PA
CBHW071438150426
43191CB00008B/1173